Light Love ~ Angels from Heaven
*New Generation * Inspiration*
Revolution ~ Revelation
All the Colours of Cosmic Rainbows

Sunny Jetsun

*'Sometimes the end of life comes as peacefully
as the passing of the day'.*
S. N. Goenkaji, dhamma.org

*'If you want to be free
you have to learn how to think for yourself'*
robertdavidsteele.com, #UNRIG

Exploring the Universe of the Heart
*

Light Love~Angels from Heaven
New Generation*Inspiration
Revolution~Revelation
All the Colours of Cosmic Rainbows
*

Sunny Jetsun

Books by the Same Author:

Originally Published as Ciel Rose
'Sadhu Sadhu Sadhu ~ "All Beings Be Happy" ~ Shanti Shanti'
'Trilogy of Vibrations ~ The Oneness of Life'
'Each Fragment of Life Is Sacred ~ These Are Your Children'
'Young Women Spin On Their Doorsteps At Dusk'
'Life Is Simple, Sharing ~ Loving Kindness from the Heart'
'The Universe Coming Across the River'
*

Originally Published as Sunny Revareva
'Pure Light, Cosmic*Sweet Heart ~ We've All Got Stars Inside'
'Perfect Love ~ No Mind * Star Light ~ Come Alive'
'True Freedom ~ Natural Spiritual Beauty ~
Here * Now ~ Gems of Eternity'
*

This book is arranged from Surreal notes
made from Inspirational conversations with friends
during the 2006/07 winter season, in Anjuna, Goa.
* Thank you all * Om Shanti Shanti *

Isn't the Planet a Wonderful place
and it's our home

'I've brought you the good stuff * Astral Padmophul Petals'
Perceptual, perpetual, floating in a golden lily pond ~
Finite body/mind: Immersion into Infinite formlessness.
Saw you in a dream >*< met you in a long, lovely poem.
Enlightenment *Transcendence* Liberation of Imagination
of your Memory, Ego, Form, Conditioned Identity, Patterns.
Free of Your Mind's limits, Pain; into limitless Cosmic reign.
Boundlessness and its Omkar, beingness, silence all around.
Free of the concepts of a Planet; Reality of our Mother Earth.
Universal nature as the ever ~ changing, everlasting energy.
Streams of Multi*Consciousness, being, growing in a buttercup,
daisy; don't get caught up in the Material delusion, illusion of it.
Somehow being the most Real, Realise the forest's sacredness.
Now how to do that? Amidst the swirling Maelstroms in the trees.
Gusting,Tantric thrusting of your desires. Just to be ~ to be frees.
Expressions now, Creation's art, feeling it in my sub*atomic heart.
Let the mind, body go as rocket boosters, falling away in free flight.
"Senility is wasted on most people", put it into Cosmic Consciousness.
Lost the Yangste Dolphin today, context; extinct gone forever, where?
No more Karma ~ becoming part of the Universal Ocean ~ here now.
Fighting with your mother's cancer, its existence, frequency ~
Realise your own true beingness and her Infinite Spirituality.
Let the big Attachments go ~ know that we're all Radiant flow.
There's innumerable disorders on Earth, to suffer them or not?
Naturally, epigenetic and those conditioned by Ignorance, Karma.
See mid-pages of WHO. ICD-10 Mental and behavioural disorders.
People amongst us are living with these, knowing and unknowing.
Affecting every one of us in our Environment ~ our Relationships.
We can't control it all; it's happening but by being Conscious of it,
empathise, put it into perspective! Whatever happens we are All
part of a greater Cosmic, boundless Consciousness. Accept that,
let it go, know mind, body is not your deeper essence ~ being flow
"Mentally-illusory because it's all coming from your limited thoughts!"

<u>Neurological (Emotional * Physical * Psychic) Disorders et al.</u>
These disorders being put into the context of a 'Zero Tolerance'
An usurper or despotic Characteristic - for those with the Power
to destroy cultures, putting all innocent lives to nuclear swords!
Effecting all Species, our DNA. strands, infinite nature; from our
neighbors, partners, children, teachers, pope, President, Mother,
Father, your favorite celebrity to influencing a light Star from afar!
This World is paying a high Price, Mother Nature is paying for our
ubiquitous fears, traumas, insatiable greed, nightmares, disorders.
How would most of us ever know or be able to comprehend the
effects of this on our beings, nerves, emotions, actions, feelings?
Don't allow any Sociopath to be the next Emperor. Did someone ever
diagnose the Brain of Lenin or 'Visionary Mind-set' of Chairman Mao?
Did we ever Psychoanalyze the decisions of Hitler, Nixon, Kissinger,
or any other country's hero; was Napoleon a well-adjusted General?
What about Pol Pot, Genghis Khan a fine Empire builder or Caesar1,
another glorious bringer of Civilisation to Barbarians living peacefully
along undiscovered pagan coasts. What is Mind, ego, this creature?
Buddha had an answer, Jesus and Krishna gave excellent advice
on the reigns of terror falling and cluster bombs dropping from the
sky on your beloved family! Creating hereditary codes which we still
live with; designing our epigenetic, karmic, deep sub-consciousness!
"I thought I saw a Dinosaur eating my wife." "Don't freak out o"
Lie on your back and look into the clear night sky to get a sense
of how **You** are the way You are; Who and Why; ~ What to do?
We are born into this state, we even bring it with us for R/evolution..
There is this undercurrent, Magma effecting all of us, take a look at its
potential '<u>disorders</u>', their <u>countless</u> links and subsections, bubbling up
Consciously/Unconsciously in us and in all those life forms amongst us,
effecting us, destroying us, loving you & me in Cosmic Quantum fields ~
Allowing this reality; 10% we think we know, what about 90% of the rest?
'What the Bleep', what about **Transcendence** of this Omnipresent Mind
to realise our true Omniscience? Enjoy that butterfly affecting your eye ~

Serving the Life

Our brain is a Computer * Meta-data, binary codes!
Reprogramming this finite Mind with, No-Mind stuff.
The yakking Mind, tell it to shut up! All is transient ~
Live from the Heart Not your Self-possessed Mind.
Mystics quieting their Mind, silencing a wild Stallion.
Pulling the reigns, Start/Stop, talking to the Senses
through our Intelligence, clear eyes * into their Spirit.
By-Pass the filter of the Mind and be naturally Pure.
How to deal with the Beggar? Sharing life's moments.
'A Tree of Life is Giving Life' ~ still growing to the skies.
Tree of Knowledge, Good and Evil, dualistic Potentials.
Osmosis, planting ~ Analysis of the moment, changing.
Screw the money, enslavement; who's creating for Life?
Who told You that You are naked Sire, or a slave mate?
Moving into the Dimension of Perception, interpretation.
"MIND SHUT UP" that which exists, omniscient in Space.
'Being in this World but not of it', all a phantasmagoria!
The purest light ~ leaving the body * a Celestial entity.
A new language from old words and odd precepts,
Identifications, Ego Conditionings, Matrix Programs.
Mind disciplined ~ Altruism supports the ones below.
Have to trick the Mind, training a wild animal potential.
Staying out of the World, out of the dramas Arjuna.
Bliss Is here and now ~ coming to us on divine wind.
Keep following light, appearing from you, before you.
Don't listen to Your limited thoughts, living in infinity.
Can You Be Aware ~ "What you see is temporal,
what you can't see is eternal." An omnipresent sail.
My Spectrum seeing the codes through a holy veil.
Simple ~ You have to be, a Receiver to Receive ~
Loving Compassion ~ moving into any dimension
where there are no words; more LIGHTS dancing

3

You can be yourself ~ You can always be your happy self
Democracy Shows, Sensors, always being watched mate!
It doesn't matter who's in Power they all do what they want.
Sociopathic ego, get to work! They didn't want us to realise
what's going on in the Matrix Mind. Accept taxing Conditions!
Possessing is more Depressing, full of Dispiriting Possibilities.
Very Greedy, fascist country; paying stealth charges to breathe!
Rules, Regulations, Licenses, fines, by laws, prison for everything.
A Public poster on the underground, "You can't beat the computer"
"You can't Escape the Computer, Pay your Car Tax." Dystopia!
The Criminal Justice Bill, Cultural effects! Surveillance brother.

*

More Optical Illusions
Himalayan Blue Bells and Rhododendrons.
Received it as a seeming Miracle, a Blessing.
Into the light energy, vortex with a Merkababy.
A free Party ~ on the beach
golden sister

*

Ein-Stein Racers & Le Grand Guignol
Slitting the fuckin' Atom in face of helping People!
Psy-ops split the personality * infinite dimensionality.
Neo-Nazionality, Oligarchy's committed UK. Asylum.
Refugees legal, Illegal living with Razor Wire Fences.
Next door - Enforcing Nationality Act, Global Accents.
Check out what's on the Bildeberger Group Menu! And
the Sovereign Military Order of Malta, U.N. Observers!
What about my new friend from the Nesara Project?

*

Base Jumping into Soft Powder
Free diving, free surfing, free falling, free energy.
Into one big Con after another; broke the O zone
Barrier. Pablo Neruda drew a map of Abstract Art.
Materialistically free ~ to reach into new dimensions

<u>It's Now or Never ~ Forever</u>
Flower seeds of Life ~ Symbolic within the Eye.
Frequency ~ wavebands and Magical art in your Heart.
In your Mind making Storm troopers from Loving Angels.
Being Objective about all this Materialisation, Ego Realm.
Frequencies of an Earthquake, a healthy disease of death.
Light radiating particles of Mind giving you Senses of ~
Identification, Values, effects, what you crave as a slave!
Radionics effecting Pyramidal, Electro Magnetic Cosmos
Ultimately common doh * Not from Chemtrail companies.
Healthy Immunity systems ~ Perfect balance with nature
and vice versa, in order to receive the Highest Knowledge.
Intuition of Universal self
*

<u>Portrait of a Pope, King Inspiring Fear Not Love!</u>
To all who see it ~ will lay in front of you, their - Power!
Commissioned to Personify the Perfection of a Madonna.
Divine Serenity in Human flesh; not more Ignorant Violence,
afire from Perugia but Sfumato tones of love's ecstatic desire.
*

<u>La Fornarina ~ Fecundare</u>
Raphael's Renaissance, he offered her a Myrtle leaf ~
Sexual fertility awakening within the Ruby Rings of Love.
Transcending her translucent erotica, his transparent exotica.
"Secret pleasures beyond all measures of the richest treasures"
Cupid's arrows flying through a holy Roman Villa.
Afterglow rumble ~ free Space, do what you want.
*

<u>Indian Rock</u>
'Thank God!' for Losing Sense..
With Reality ~
"I want to Live on an Abstract Plane."
Vieni qui

Virtual ME Not DNA. (Serial Barcode- #)
"Just gave my Name, Rank and Social Insurance No"
"Get Away from that Bone!" Hi-Tech alloy of a hybrid clone.
Modern Abstract Art, "What do you see Mother?" It's a drone!
Natural, "a big Orange blob", grazie to Cy Twombly, sincerely.
Not living inside the Matrix, an Invisible Prison; now free ~
More Smart Powers ~ A. I. to be.
No own Hell, No I destined to die.
Cosmic eye's Vibrational energy ~
Bluest Sky * frequencies of Infinity
*

New Crest
Piss head draining ~ another Clear Reflection * Priapus'
Lotus Pond not Vampires masquerading in squires' attire.
Our sweetest coitus through hot nights, Inspiring carnal fires.
Opening to responding; how will your Mania comprehend,
'to be or not to be', or to be both here & at the same time.
Why or Why Not? Or don't think about it and for Always ~
*

Puppet Masters with a Global Veto
Found 'The Haliburton Agenda' still clicking under a radioactive bush…
"9/11 continues with images that some of our viewers might find distressing."
Pause for Station Identification; realised no one would believe Rebekah Roth.
*

Mr. & Mrs. Democratius
Nature Free and Perfect ~ Man Manicured, She's botoxed.
Unocal, Enron, BP, Shell, then there's Gen. Colin Powell.
"What we're giving you is fact and conclusions based on
solid Intelligence." 2/2001. Ok, let's start a War brother!
We'll make them live in an aura of endless threat and fear.
Spouted out by a self-confessed hypocrite. "Wouldn't you,
My fellow Americans rather resign than be dishonored?"
The Independent Voice of the People choked to death.

<u>Nishargadatta's Satsinging ~ "I Om in Om"</u>
Cosmic rays flooding my greenhouse's living room.
Those groovy Vibes Vibing ~ not War pinging, ding!
Serendipity's synchronicity ~ at least respect humanity.
A compassionate view not political dancing in Botafago.
Tathagatta: "I can't give Dhamma to anyone in Chains."
"We've paid a high price for Freedom; one Million dead at
the Inner gates of frozen, starving Leningrad, Comrade."
Gone to Mars with Jellybeans in a psychedelic nutshell.
Free trance music! Sometime ~ got to leave the Rock.
Inmates ~ got to let the rock roll, let the sword fall away.
Inside our own heads we have the Potential to fly high,
becoming transformational; Insight is ~ Right here now.
Try to reduce the Chaos. Who Loves a Tyrant and why?
Accepting their Condition. A system's implicit threat of being
watched all the time with the Inevitability of being Punished!
*
<u>We go to War to demand Peace</u>
Needing to QUIT this Mindset ~ Mind's deeper Matrix.
Karma, "We all pay for each other in the favela sister"
Fear controls these people but eventually changes!
"How the hell do You die in a Crossfire on the street?"
Meditating, we're Capable of ~ All I heard was Chaos.
"As long as we live in a War Zone our Ideology
won't allow us to be passive and live in comfort.
Sweating Lambada with a temptress, Maria Gasolina.
A sea spirit asked me to come & talk to a broken body."
"Then I felt the Greatest Happiness"
"You'll have to work through this Barrier of Pain."
"I am a Warrior of the People"
What we create and destroy is passed through generations.
Going down and making offerings to the Ocean Goddess ~

Allies of Humanity
"I don't like my phone talking back to me."
The Conditioned State; I don't believe anything!
There's no clock in Goa, throw that thing away!
Meditation ~ Stop the voices in the head...
Disidentify; just the thoughts in your mind.
"It's only the Space that remains!"
*

Everything went Psychedelic
They're not in the energy of the music ~
only dancing, posing with their favourite DJs,
then going upstairs to have another line!
A billion rainbows in every raindrop.
Down a load of acid and see what happens!
*

Cognitive Dissonance
"I'm not here to please anyone, I'm here to please myself!"
"By nature, why do you want to capture it when it's free?"
Let it be. Mixing the law of the land with the law of the sea'
If you get a lawyer you're fucked; you're fucked anyway!
"90% of US. prisoners are in jail voluntarily. If you don't
know the law they'll take you to the cleaners. They can
only prosecute a dead person, if you go in there and tell
them you're alive, you'll see the Judge jump out the window!"
The lawyer works for the court, giving away your jurisdiction.
"No, you're not a gangster because you listen to rap music!"
It's about self-ownership, you're in your own trust mate"
I am that I am, chain of command, causes chain of reaction.
Heard In speeches, "do as I say, not, do as I do" Thoughts!
Absolutely no 'definitions' but please don't have a stroke!
Tricks of the mind; brainwashing your self into believing it.
"They're all laundering it." "You need to get out of town!"
"Don't let them take you alive!"
"I don't trust the clouds"

Kaleidoscopic 3D Stencils
As a matter of fact, "even strumpets have feelings."
Dyspraxic, not perceiving >< Mortises & Tenons!
"Direct Spatial experience ~ got it firsthand"
"Anjuna, off your head, in the right way…
not down in the gutter trying to get a fix"

*

Standing Back
"I don't want to Control but others want to control us"
I'll get wound up but not so caught up in it anymore…
Anything ~ Love, Beauty, hate, ugliness is in the Mind,
eyes, tongues of beholders. Stuff going on all the Time ~
don't want to Block, be Judge-mental, being resistance.
Resonating out ~ got a train ticket to Ootacamund

*

Goa Exempt
It's the Freedom
to be ~
Your Self
to accept not except ~ every one's freedom.
"I'm goin' there and I'll be Happy…
neural catalysts, electric impulses effecting moods

*

Trust that doesn't return
Don't want to lose it.
A Cultural thing ~
The News Dictates
how we behave
What we think…
rather than going out and meeting people…
Expectations ~ Why turn your other cheek?
"He got over it"
I Understand
Now ~

"It's Against the Law to Help Terminally Ill People Die
But we can Drop Bombs on them and their Children!"
Adam's Intuition ~ why leave Paradise Pussycat?
Why leave heavenly Eve? Your free choice ~
Something happened, something changed.
Came to the Pyramids, "Can't bear this!"
A baby picking up a falling coconut….
blew up in his hand in a Cosmic garden!

*Mind * Mirror*
"Does Analytical mean critical, ironical darling?
I don't want any promises, just a ride to Hilltop.
Always Wondering what you're thinking
in your lovely, blue eyes ~
*
Cog's view of an Indian train
A rolling TB. Petrie dish ~
Unplug >>> Free Wheeling
*
Happy Christmas
"Do you want a drop?"
Everyone gave me drugs…
"It's nice when everyone is tripping"
MDMA. makes everybody Happy
which is lovely, having FUN.
"I didn't expect this!"
We are alive, then we see
other things Alive ~
Vote with your Heart, putting your head through rainbows.
The Mind Outside is a reflection of what is inside ~ new Sun.
A happy, perfect day, Venetian doors opening into Intuition.
With a Mayan Calendar we're all linked to Cosmic Moons.
Pulling in the Ocean in your veins, in your blood ~

A Wife is not a Domestic Appliance no matter what!
Transcend all the desire in your heart AND Celebrate life.
Transcend all feelings on your body, all ideas in your Ego-mind.
Transcend all dreams and Illusions in your imagination
Transcend all vibrations from your nose to ~ your toes.
Transcend all karma in your subconscious thought stream.
Transcend all contact with cause and effect, be here now ~
Mystical experiences reacting to flashes of neurological
stimulation. Stuck an electromagnet on the Lama's head
for out of body sensations, feeling in direct contact with
divine power, so the scientists said, when he left hospital!
*
'Being watched all the time becomes part of Consciousness ~
Social control with right technology; Our Artificial Virtual Reality.
"You don't need to watch everyone if everyone believes they're
being watched. Punishment isn't necessary but the Inevitability
of punishment has to be programmed into the brain." Foucault.
Have you read 'The Traveller', p.174 by J. Twelve Hawks?
"Stay in the present she told herself. She tried not to think
about what had happened. Concentrate on each action,
avoid the distraction." (New 1984!) p.193, 'The Traveller'.
Listening to your conversations, tracking your purchases.
People pretending it's not true, not happening. Biometrics,
profiling, surveillance cameras, government data-basing.
People rejecting the vast machine, the coercion, Imprints.
Your embedded * Data-destroying viruses, Computationally.
Immunology programs, breaking down your smart firewalls.
"Why are you still keeping me against my Free will?" Citizen!
'Knew she was a Prisoner in Dachau, everything she wanted
but Freedom to leave. "I'm Not frightened of You" Persecutor.
"For People by the People", not for despotism, Totalitarianism,
Autocratic Fascism. Like caged animals, People have to think ~
about being Prisoners. The animal lost its memory of Freedom.
Her last word, 'Liberté'

11

Eclipsing
Fell in Love with his wife who was a gangster,
fell from another galaxy into a Beijing garden.
She was that sublime Jasmine lady of shared destiny ~
Once ripped from her family, sold into diabolic slavery,
her spirit reappeared in an anonymous Tantric painting.
Opening to the World she flew away as a Purple butterfly.
This mystical warrior survived and found the road home.
Disguised crouching tiger looking for her hidden dragon.
A mythological heroine with beautiful, deep expressions,
within the eyes of a Princess, living as a Cosmic legend.
I found her in my heart ~ a Geisha touching the starlight.

*

Prana Hemispheres
Revealing, receiving blisses of kisses
beings from other spaces
in between your eyes ~
in between your flirting, cheeky smile,
in between your wet, pink petal lips.
Pollinating a pouting Universe

*

Indescribable
'Your mind is the cycle of births and deaths ~ Samsara'.
Sri Ramana Maharshi, talk 31. & Your writing is painting,
when those energetic symbols come through your hand.
"I'll never forget the sound of that lady hitting the windscreen!"
"Don't think you can just turn up, pillage and plunder our village!"
On her way to catch terrorists, what's more important than that?
'Like a mad man trusting us with the keys to his new house.'
"I am not only the eye that hears, the ear that sees; I am"
feeling the experience, allowance, eternal essence of now.
When narcissist, bipolar girl marries ADD. Dyspraxic man!
Off her rocker Loving Krishna, full on infatuation.
Symptoms, syndromes & disorders of living Tao

<u>Found the Holy Vedas in Vegas with Bunny</u>
"Welcome to the fuckin' jungle Maitreya!"
Found the others pissing in the Church,
he beat him with a hammer! Brother.
Busted for a scam of the Mafia, Opening up a can of conditioning!
"He's forgiven in the Name of the Father, son and holy phantom"
Catholic Church, Jesuits, the Mob, the Corporations in Control!
Put some more blue ointment in it! Always has some Pay Off.
She wears the pants, he wears a cassock, the purple, gold gown.
"watched him before the sanctimonious wall came tumbling down"
"We don't like them, they slaughtered my family many years ago!"
The dry old guard is still in Power! Now I can speak my Mind ~
"Now I can learn to see the figment of my Mind for what it truly is"
*

<u>Breeding Time</u>
"I don't wanna hear other people's sob stories!"
"I can't help but Love the bitch, not into any denial of my feelings"
Bringing a baby into the World to live under a tarpaulin with me!"
Trying not to think about it, going with the flow; screaming for mercy!
"If you need a multi*dimensional Orgasm give me a ring ~ Free form".
Right, wrong, even for a Dalai Lama is altruistic Consciousness.
"We all die, you die wise or you die as a cunt!"
*

<u>Always Changing</u>
New Inspiration, Revolution, Rebirthing Elements.
"If you sit on the grass and sleep in the orchard ~
you always want to go back and smell the flowers.
We shouldn't lose those natural things ~
that's the moment, that's what it's all about"
Feeling to do it now ~ no time-frame within the Mind.
Giving oneself up to this moment, no doubt, needing it.
Being here with no past memories, no imaginary future.
"How was it in the foetal, not fatal position? As it is ...
"Let There Be Light"

13

"It could be You", is an 'Archetypal' Ad. Slogan!
Different Views < 360 secs. * Time & angle > Positions ~
Getting a fleeting glimpse, feelings of Intuitive knowledge!
"You agree to live in the hive, take what the hive dishes out"
"All Boxed up and ready to go." Very clever trick, deceit!
That's why the Hyperboreans are covered in Sunshine ~
and that's why they came up with Surrealism to explain
'Women's Psyches'. What about hearts & moist pussies?
Mine's beating in a rainbow covered hearse in Havana.
We're all Interlopers here; Welcome to Martian Utopia.
Cartoons of God, Issues of Freedom, being able to say
what we want. Who says we can't & why? Lost your Id!
Too busy to recognise the stars, the trees, the flowers,
the animals, the sea, mother nature, even the children!
Sensing the wet rain falling, sensing the concept of Tao ~
Inside & outside the same, there is No Separation of bits.
If you torture my friend you torture me, General Tyranny.
If your Militias starve those refugees, you destroy us all.
Expanding * timeless ~ limitless* Universe after Universe.
"Natural is Supernatural" ~ Not only words. Care not Scare.
Just observe the sensations don't get caught up in 'Identity'
In the Identification of it, so Attaching Itself to some 'Value'
reflected in you, your ego, so this cause, causes a reaction.
This contact creates a cycle of being ~ makes sense to me.
"What happens inside, happens outside me too and you ~
It is all One without an ego or even with an ego * Feeling.
Effortlessness of Cosmic rays, you blossoming into days.
All together beating in Brahma's heart

*

Spot the Bomb at the Predatory Bank
Dr. Crippen who are these people…
who see 'Success' in War and death?
This is Capitalist America-Time is Money!
'Low level mercury Tuna is better for you'.

Fact of Life ~ Fact of Illusion
Thank you for reminding me again ~ that Love Conquers All.
"Sometimes you have to destroy someone you Love to move
forward with your own life." She had to hate me, to leave me!
"You picked me up off the street and gave me your blood!"
"You're projecting your anxieties, don't worry, be here NOW.
You don't do snorting? Only snorkeling mate!
Star Jasmine, "Run, maybe you will live!"
*

Doctor from Dahomey
'A thin blue giant sensed me'
There are people of different colours who
held my hand and said, "You're going to Live!"
"Tout va bien, tout va bien." "I was in tears…
*

Magical Brahma
"Very interesting with the Alien"
"beginningless, incomprehensible, indescribable,
ever transforming all the elements as one, being ~
an integral part of the great continuum of all that is"
Psychic sweets of Cosmic No Knowing ~
Facing Amazing clear, cerulean auras
*

Galileo's Law of Falling Bodies ~ definition.
Very psychedelic couple in a graffitied canoe.
Pointing to the twinkling stars off red, ruby Mars.
"Why does it have to be Concentric ~ Your holiness?"
Reflections always slipping between the veils of light ~
Velvet expressions tripping under ripples in the sand.
*

*Happy Marriage * Happy Mirage*
You know what long term delirium is?
"What's the secret?" "Two words!"
"Yes Dear" ~ be Your 'True self'

15

Omnificence
Brain Chatter...
Hard self poor trait
Context, telling a story.
Nothing is on its own ~
Together as a concept of Surreal, Tantra Kundalini
especially with the added dimension of Realisation.
Different reflections shine out of an abstract window.
Feeling from here, inside to there, outside.
Unity of the continuom of moments ~
*
Honduras Street
* Deep Space Molecules *
'Can't get to the end of it ~
because there is NO end to it!
Realising she didn't Know any better.
Can you forgive that excuse? I hope so.
Emotions caught in a conflicting narrative,
She's wearing her sweet, summer perfume.
Away from the natural to believe Perception,
and what do you call Unconscious, my Cherie?
It's supposed to happen ~ accepting that; It is this.
Meant to be this because IT'S happening right now.
Now the rest is all Illusion, isn't that right Mayadevi?
"You smell a pakora it pulls you in", said a Rishi...
*
"Man Up Baba!"
Being Happy ~ with the Time
"The past is history * the future a mystery
and the now ~ is a gift"
'That's why it's called the Present'
Take your Mind off it, they'll be gone.
"It's Killing Me!"

The Queanie
'I'm just in your head'
The Bees do all the work,
You just collect the Honey!
"All you need is Love ~
All You need is to Share Love"
Did you ever read, 1984, Animal Farm, or
The Murder of Princess Diana; Brave New World?
In Konkani, "My chappels Baba; left them out, not here?"
Out of Respect; "someone took them, I lost my chappels."
"Did you ask me to look after your chappels?"
"Am I not in your house?" ~ Its very nature...
*

Through & Through
The Sound Barrier
The Crash Barrier
The Light Barrier
The Class Barrier
The Pain Barrier ~
Mind's thresholds
*

Be Here Now
Focus on the Love.
Optional Stress
If we don't choose it ~ It's not there.
"It might be legal to stick people in ovens
But it's not right!"
"Do you know what I mean?"
*

Not to Worry, Waving again
A Stream of Consciousness ~ passing
throughout ~ Your Conditioned ego/mind/brain.
'In the Process' of making ~ a proper decision.

Free Tibetan Culture of the World
Discovery of the Moon landing or/on the Nature of the Mind?
Eternal Humanity, Ocean of Wisdom, Om Mani Padma Hum.
Corrupt Powers do nothing again ~ except make Proxy wars!
Free to move, but my Mind's Imprisoned Itself. Feel beyond ~
Is this Ancient Knowledge worth protecting, to you, humility,
or do you allow for Genocide, Inhumanity, to predominate?
Mega Predators congregating at a Proto Nazi Rock concert!
Left them to be, Slaves and Prisoners and forgotten corpses,
while you still play games in your self-indulgent, UN. talk shops!
Getting well paid, living in a Luxurious World of delusion.
Making reasonable excuses for its behaviour since 1948.
OPEN MIND *OPEN YOUR MIND* AND CONSCIENCE.
Your Self Importance to Peoples' Realities of Suffering!

*

B O * O M
Giving more Entrepreneurs; beg me for a startup!
A way out of Poverty, to work for themselves…
"We are designed to eat meat."
"Oh really!" "Are you the designer?"
Misrepresenting, 'Conditioned Carnivores'
What you can do is to become ~
* C O N S C I O U S *
"To dispel the darkness…
simply switch on the light"
"See It" ~ then you'll believe It.

*

Momentom
Clear Mental State…
Knowing, Not Knowing
what's gonna happen ~
And you take it from there….

Chicks on Sunbeams
Exhaust fumes & plastic swords blowing big bubbles,
speeding trains of photons on atomic spinning sticks ~
Dolce Vita feeling the base, Party of your Personality.
'Soul' searching Mecca for a unique piece of meteorite.
Even had many wars there, recognising Full, Fire Power!
Full Sun * waking from a trance in a beach Temple, of Goa.
*

Praise the Lord, Pass the Ammo!
Would it be too much to ask them to shut the F… up about it?
"Remember the Alamo!" for some, "Happy December 7th"
"Lock and Load!" "I feel my cock chakra straighten out."
"Miss Kitty's Eco*echo Star was closed to the Menace
so we went to the Electric Lotus for a Munch fruit!
"Bring it on!" She could have just stood there…
and I would have given her money!"
*

DESIGNER STRESS
'Too hasty to resist'
Another Affluent Mental Brand.
Reacting Unconsciously ~
Seeing the Insane as Sane!
*

'Strategists ~ the Penalty of Celebrity'
"You're always isolated from the people you want to be with."
"The Dalai Lama as was the Pope, holding up a Theocrazy.
He's the unique one who got away, others had to stay!
Had the Inside view and the Power to survive in luxury.
Lives in 5* Palaces, peasants are in the Suffering fields.
1st class travel, best of things and international applause.
Picked from outside a Ruling Class; No Wars of Succession."
I don't believe it myself brother; he's an altruistic human being

Sitting on an Obelisk
Fear or Love? She left me utterly broken and empty ~
Out of that nothing is the essence of all life existence.
The law of nature is same same different everywhere.
Liberated enlightenment, transcend your limited mind,
any dark energy, to have Awareness of eternal SPACE
(Mastery over Your Mind's delusions!)
You have to Know its nature, conditions.
You have to see it objectively ~
What its nature is, ego wants.
To realise It, being beyond it ~
Seeing through it all
*

You Perceive it
Should You not then have Feelings?
Addicts ~ hooks in from a pussy's claws!
Instinct based on him getting his end away.
Addiction is hard to get any grip of…
*Time Heals * Time Feels*
"Did that really happen?"
*Let that Spark * enlighten*
the Flame ~
No Control, I didn't think about it.
I was in ~ 'I know now
let it go, believe me,
don't need to know'
*

The Awareness
Fully Embrace
Intuitive Love ~
Need to be Independent
need to come back to
*Your * self*

<u>Detachment of a forlorn love</u>
It's being above it ~
Inspiration not Barriers.
When you're down
sharing a room…
Hate turned to Love
Something nice ~
it Started from there.
*

<u>Helicopter Surveillance</u>
Concentrated to learn Dante ~ 'The Inferno', by heart!
And learnt a few things about Paradise from Casanova.
Sound of a very special nymphet's or strumpet's address?
You're Alive in my heart ~ "I miss you"
Wiped out all the Memories ~
"Nothing better happen to this child!"
"They don't care what you think, if you're exiled Outside."
*

*<u>Code * A gift</u>*
Mind Reading, a program on brainwashing.
"I can FEEL What You're Thinking"
Yes I like It very much >< Intuition*
They erased her memories, wiped it clean.
Why would they > took away her eggs…
they knew she was guilty of something!
"I'll stay with you until you wake up darling."
In My dreams ~ stories of Magic & Adventure,
"I was there, before we were transported…
now we're prisoners of our genes", the latest string.
You could have done anything there as long as you
had wanted it enough ~ 'A Pleasure to have You'.
Any Violation of the Code? "Alaikum Salam."
Regulations: Rules: Proclamations: Fatwahs.
Arriving at the full Moon festival of Sphinxes

Terrible burning
Cost of Living Today. Our Pensioner's in dire straits ~
Water, Electric, Gas bills and exorbitant Council Taxes!
Spending a life-time, spending money, wasting Power resources.
Ash to ash, dust to dust, Cosmic energies into Cosmic frequency ~
Nestle's draining our aquafers, don't you know by now? Never Mind!

*

Stand Well Back
Intuitive to your true nature, Alex Grey, Ramana Maharshi Yogi.
Going through a Mind freely, Maharaji ~ Sadhguru, Mooji.
Making beedies in the afternoon with Nisargadatta*Shri.
Sunny mango, Life Is Simple, Sharing Living Kindness,
Sharing Loving Kindness, from the heart'
Let go the breath ~ the key, 'desire less desire'
"I will Never Abandon You" ~ Om Krishna Hari.

*

Envisaging
Behind the story, behind the theory, beyond their glory.
Envisaging the Mind for what it is, all its Characteristics ~
what I then am, a man, womb*man, conscious beingness.
'Seeing the Mountain from the distance' * the Lotus Lily,
'the fairest of them all' is about to change ~ Unfolding.
A powerful Frenzy <:> My Mind its Self-perpetuating.
Feeds itself on itself for itself, survival Instincts of aeons.
Mind/body contact, doing the blind reacting of thoughts,
Bio*chemically, electro*magnetically, sustenance, force.
Any thought you want and innumerable never imagined!
Changing every instant generating alternating energies ~
Keeps feeding the conscious vibe, Quantum life streams.
Ego's volition feeding ~ its very own meaning.
Be Your*self completely

*

India ~ Goa Lite…
Goa Smiles ~ every day's hippie happy

Kali DNA. Strands

Texas Honky-tonks of God, man and...
Animal man turning around the four walls.
"Make the World go Away!"
Didn't want to fall into the trap of society.
Shamans surfing on a smoking Thai stick ~
Building light works * Indian Jasmine refractors.
Just a mind-game but everything is Consciousness.
Even opposites integrated in the here and now ~
All the movies have stopped ~ Brahma is present
*

Respire * Inspire

Complete Prasad Cosmic food, 'No Prana No Life'
Going with the flow of all the people, my family
are in the same mouthful ~ in the same breath.
Incomprehensible < * > God please spare me,
get me out of this suffering, I'm in desperation...
They left you for dead! An Om in us * Potent being.
Space is open now, seeing through mental-process.
Going through the materialism using Truth's Platform.
Telepathic waves, vibrational, synchronicity symphony.
Allows it into the right, light frequency; have to change,
can't live in that old state with absolutely no sympathy ~
EMF. wavelengths cooking brains. Know it, you're better
at navigation than migratory birds with PhD's in weather.
Necessity not Accessory < 'The Struggle' > for Survival.
Conceived sensations which give Insight to carry On.
It gives the Mindfulness that this suffering will arrive ~
one day or another for most of us. How to embrace it?
The Best bubbling Protection in the Universe ~ 'Panna'.
How to deal with an unbelievable accident, divorce, lies,
miscarriage, loss, invasion, violent death? Take your pick.
The Brahma Vihara is in Your Qualities of Loving Kindness,
Compassion, Sympathetic Joy and Equanimity ~ Liberation.

King of Eugenic Elves

Terrortorial > What happens when the CO_2 bubble bursts?
Splash, splotch, plop, pop! ~ And you are very, very hurt…
Pain and Fear ~ be Happy dear with no personal attachment.
How to keep the body and Mind Calm? From not cracking up!
Vipassana is stillness, practice focusing on a vibrational Path ~
In Silence ~ Your Mind's characteristics, developing balance

*

Koran * Sutra 27

The walk around a Sacred Place ~ Sacred Landscape.
A garden in the desert, on a clear, full Moon, night sky.
"Even the most beautiful things are transient"
'wisdom when their violent passions are spent'
"Not a Woman but a World"
His heart was with her, they met in Africa.
She arrived on her Emerald silk Magic carpet ~
first saw her in an early morning Incense market.
Genies burning Myrrh ~ Perfume for her Gods.
Worshipping the Sunlight at the Port of Kana.
Making Love in warm depths, of her moist, lush
Wadi ~ very sweetly, singing the songs of Poets.
Traveling together on Caravans of 20,000 nomads.
Happy spirits willing that it happened ~ great isn't it!

*

Simultaneously from the Minaret

Another Invitation to a beheading and chop Ancient trees!
Enhancement, how to keep sane with an Aluminium brain?
"The Mind is a Primal Operating System for its Own Self-ends"
Always there, wants Transhumanism, bio-evolution is too slow!
Awareness of that distinct Mind ~ naturally
by concentration, on being free, truly, simply.
Accept everything as it is ~ as a part of this reality.
No need to feel any Separation from a bumble bee.
Breathing in the Cosmic connection ~

Psy*Chics Initiation story
Entering the realm of death.
Saved by a Divine woman ~
whose lover he must become.
Swears to be ever True to her.
Apollo made the Island rise up.
Their gods don't allow many
to live happily ever after.
The dark and Cruel side
Offering of a beautiful young Princess,
they broke their promise to the Temple.
Her Crime was Pure ~
A statue to the women…
Suffering, simply known as the Terror-Inquisition!
"Can fool some of the Oracles all of the Time
All of the Oracles some of the time ~
but not all of the Oracles, all of the time."
His destiny had been fulfilled.
Killed by their Gods ~
lying by the seashore
*

Metro-Link
"We're gonna wait for a moment ~
We're waiting for a passenger from the other side."
"I believe that's everybody ~
Please stand clear, doors are closing"
*

'Imperfect'
Grammatically expressing action as Continuous
and not completed ~ 'the becoming of Reality'
Levels of Intuition

<u>Psychopathic Technocrats</u>
They're trying hard to screw you and your Mind!
Don't know any better, beating their pissed off, hysterical wife!
Who beats their children, their mongrel dog with Bio-weapons?
Mass culling; who drops rockets into your school's playground?
There's Microbes, cancers, diseases, viruses, strokes; Predators.
Who works with eugenicists, fornicators, detractors, Inspectors?
Invasion of Biosphere Space ~ by someone's Android I phone!

*

<u>Let's go to the Del Mar Fair</u>
Wheelers and dealers in every crook and cranny.
Accepted as a Winning Streak on Your Race Card!
No room for any Freak show, their Aphrodisiac is Power!
Plastic surgery technology; fashionistas on a grand scale.
Steroid Testosterone, fueled male at a Grand sale.
Taken to its Max, going on to make a gruesome War.
Accepting own serfdom, need to fill the Company store!
"I wouldn't know a soul you know"
"Eat your heart out", she said!
Why be Terrified at all?

*

<u>Broken Arrow Cameo</u>
The Mind doing its thing in the foreground, always there.
As an Observer it's really weird, the toughest shit ~
Disharmony, in the Ignorance of pain and suffering.
A disaster for you, your Mind, coming in a Kit-Form
but Transcendence is alive, if you can accept it, not sterilization!
As a Big lesson ~ going through enhanced Ego barriers of Wo*Man.
No more mind's thoughts, no more separation, no more life or death,
entering here and now, amidst divine atoms of the Cosmos.

*

<u>Arturius of Iona</u>
"He fell in a swoon, Ah!
Now I have my death ~

26

Pure Grail Myth
The Quest, symbol of Virtue and Equality; my Lord.
Not another bloody, Royal tailbone, a reborn Taliban!
What's in the Minds of those Warmongering Politicians?
Needed a Reformation, Royal decree, a revolution brother!
Crystallising our dreams inside a cowrie shell ~
Explosion of the Legend, breaking the hypnotic Spell!
Focus for a Spiritual Reawakening beside a sacred well.
In fields of bluebells under Glastonbury's splendid Tor.
We met and loved each other ~ until the end of our days.
Being with you in the Age of Angels

*

Ocean of Angels
No origins of reality just imaginary?
Medieval mysticism and Ancient Alchemy…
A hero made from the hands of Celtic Bards.
Red Dragons battling White Dragons.
"I Know the depth of every lake"
through Poetry and Prophecy
of Merlin's Magic

*

Otherwise Our Igurna
A Castle by the seashore ~ Ocean surf crashing.
"If I do not possess her I will go Mad with desire."
Like to see the light sparkling in her eyes ~
to know that it's all magnificently real, mine!
Sent her an sms. "Already high in Venice"
Should give you a good heads up to their condition.
A calibration proceedure; while balmy summer air ~
breezes through scented bushes of vivid, pink Bougainvillea.
Sweet, coquettish expressions on Zhang Ziyi's butterfly wings.
'Satya' ~ a golden Spiritual Age of being together with you.

~ Osho ~
Ancient Japanese first used by Eka to address his master
Boddhidharma. 'O' means with great respect, gratitude,
love, as well as synchronicity and harmony. 'Sho' means
'multi*dimensional expansion of consciousness'.
An 'existence showering from all directions'

*

Paying through the Nose > Attitude
Lost in raging storms of ego, Yobs and Squires; jolly what!
The countryside is nice but I don't like the people much.
Patronising Elitism and "Wo' Yu Lookin' at Yu Wanker?"
"Fuckin' piss off then", she said. Not so phlegmatic, Brits!
Neo-fascist negativities >culture of an Empire in Chaos.
Ripped-off every way on a lovely day. Habitual shame.
Whining, whinging, nothing but complaining, blaming,
blame, blame, blame, guilty, shame game, like a song
from a west end musical, down at the Olde Bull & Bush!
Oh so merry, psychological Warfare on a mob by a mob,
in such a pretentious, aggressive green and pleasant land.

*

< Extremes > What's goin' on in this Brave New World?
Lost the direction ~ Children violated on every street corner,
women pissed up, lying in every gutter, living next to a nutter!
What's happened to this land, more cameras than on Grandstand!
More CCTV surveillance than the rest of the World combined…
have we lost our Mind? ASBOs, Anti-social behaviour orders
for 6 year old's with machetes and glue pipes. Police can enter
your house anytime to check if there's an illegal shed in disguise!
Parking fines and speeding tickets, tearaway teenagers, terrorists
in every kiosk, Mosque; the Psychologic drama outside a chip shop!
Has to be true, read it in the Tabloids, saw it on BBC Panorama.
Nobody mentions Our impoverished pensioners, pawning
their medals and living in a mean tested depression of fear.
Who gets £2,000,000, never says a word, just eats crisps?

King Chop
My Mind Free ~ what's that mean Socrates?
Always grows, trees giving oxygen naturally!
Naturally ~ My Mind is doing it, unconsciously
My Mind is being the causing and effecting, it.
Behaviour reflecting, reacting ~ be Subjective.
Calming my fear dear is calming my mind down,
be Objective, be the Witness, see beyond the Ego.
It's all enacted within this pantomime like a Clown.
The Stage of TV, News, soaps and Docu-dramas...
Under the controls of Authoritarian program, systems.
"Only they can save us" from their Own Mess, Anthem!
Politicians - 'Blair's a Dead Duck in the Homeland mate'
665,000 civilians killed in this Unjust, Illegal war to date!
Take a deep breath and connect to simply being ~ As it is.
*

Honorary Sun Centre & In 1663 - Space with No air
The Painter of Light, metaphor for the 'Enlightenment'.
'The Air Pump' > Creation of a Vacuum! Abhorrent!
Heresy to the One & Only; Exclusive, Theocratic Church.
"God couldn't just Create Nothing!" But that's all there is.
'The Lunar Men' and Magdeburg Spheres ~ raining,
tears & fears; "Take no one's word for it" even Ptolemy.
Unlocking the Secrets & Mysteries of nature & galaxies.
"If you're interested in what a substance does, its effect;
get rid of it and see what happens." That makes sense.
"Why do creatures breathe and fly around the Sun?"
Mr. Wright tried putting birds and mice in a vacuum!
Showed extinction and resuscitation in a candle light.
*Air, oxygen and nitrogen * bringing them back to life!*
"Your Regal Emperor the Pope, Herr Otto Von Guericke
is at the door with Science, not another Unholy Inquisition!"
"Here is the man, God has chosen to be Your King" - Seeing
your own habits, Addictions, dysfunctions, for what they are

29

<u>Your Omerta Majesty</u>
An Unlawful Killing spun-out by the media.
Misinterpreting the verdict, Sham inquest.
A Nazi background murdering them all ~
Who's married a fucking Psychopath then?
"Every camera was switched off M. Maigret!"
They'll never ever challenge the Top layer.
Unelected Power and unfettered privilege.
Ban Anti-Personnel landmines your Highness!
A DESPICABLE CRIME AGAINST HUMANITY.
"Knowledge Is Power" who said that me lud?
"They've decided I'm a non-starter,
I lead from the heart not the head.
Someone's got to go out there and Love people."
A loose cannon, 'accidents do happen, yu know!'
"I'd like to be the Queen of people's hearts"
Their family have a history of assassinations.

*

<u>TAX & the First Slap!</u>
We're used to being conned.
That's why we put up with it.
Cruelty Is Not Consciousness. Rebooting!
"Karma is only in the past or future, if you're in
the Present ~ there is no Karma." Makes sense!
Who invented the term, 'Collateral Damage'?
"Why did you bring that King cobra home dear?"
The immoral Royal treasure in an offshore tax haven!
"Do as we say, not do as we do." We're robbing you!
"You do what you believe in?" "Allahu Akbar!"
"Won all the Wars and destroyed the Planet"
People forget, a strobe flashgun, 'I AM U'
Crystal footprints * Hologram * Fractal
"I'm coming in Hot!"

Kim's little brother
"The Associations were too Painful"
Starting off for the Front Line of War!
That Terrible Telegram - 'Missing in Action'. For what?
"I will send you a Field postcard from Hell's Trenches"
Doing his duty, my boy Jack buried in Clay Pit Wood.
"No meaning to things when you lose your only son"
*

Goa Goin' Gone
Monkey see, monkey do, 55,000-volt tasers! They're deluded.
"I'm another non-starter, I lead from the heart not from the head."
Dumbing down your kids, barcodes inside baby nano-vaccines!
Chemtrails in a vibrational prison, Mind's microchips.
Who's having a war on our human immune system?
Ask the pharmaceutical cartel at your local drug store.
A mad play of Identification, "I am an Abstract Artist"
Not calling a bird a bird, being every other possibility.
When you're a little baby, WHO ARE YOU REALLY?
Look Into Your Self
*

Attention Here Is Now Intention
Pronounced Mad and sectioned for speaking outside of the Insanity ~
Be Present ~ Past, future is only karma, so part of the mental movement.
Where is Life? The only access to Life is Now, not imagination, fear & memory.
Putting us out of the flow ~ as basing it in thoughts; It's not all down to Me mate.
"It's all unconsciousness but people don't know its unconscious; think it's Normal!"
A lot of suffering, "Your biggest catastrophe is your greatest gift of enlightenment."
Not breaking the Mind, accepting it for what it is, only in fields of duality*Polarities.
Transmutation, transportations, transformation, Transcendence, Feeling ~ Reality.
Feeling it in my heart, realising compassion amidst all this continuous negativity...
Darling it happened to me, she lost it, betrayed me with lies; I took it too personally.
'They're suffering, not havin' a go at You!'

Taking Down All the Flags of Nationalism
Pure ~ soft Pink outline from a flesh Impact studio.
Changing the fires of love into a Celebratory defeat,
beyond the black mask. Another punishment shooting,
everyone's a victim in this 'Man's' world of Sovereignty.
Sent to Northern Ireland for a condoned knee capping.
Society doesn't censure artists who don't pose a danger.
You are now entering 'Free Derry', full graffiti. What are you
fighting for? Contradictions protruding from a skull in disguise.
"Beware of the Armed Dog", Ire-response-able; 'WHY ME?'
Left-overs from an old illusion; the kept-hidden wars of Oil.
What are emotions? Cannibals, slavery; perversions exist.
"We don't even know what's going on in our own minds!
An old saying, "We have met the enemy and it is us."
"You must be present to win"
*

'Emotional Landscape'
"My life has been filled with terrible thoughts
most of which never happened." Mark Twain.
*

*Automation * 10% of Mind*
Needed to justify 90% of decisions based on emotion ~
At the Supreme Court, reaction to a near miss accident!
Perspective, Awareness, Observation, Recognition ~
Nature didn't make it easy to Observe Your own Self.
"Techniques to expand Consciousness into areas,
not normally where it goes." Learning to be ~
more Attentive to you, to your fate, to your face
responding to me ~ giving a lovely, friendly smile.
*

beach comber:
'A long wave rolling in from the Ocean ~ A settler in the
Pacific Islands, living by Pearl fishing and other means'.

Pilgrimage - "Tell it to the Infantry"
Dad's Army, "Eyes Front" defending against another Blitzkrieg!
"We led the way." The Anti-personal Mines were swept away.
All marching now with the 'Limbless and Burnt Association'.
Proudly bearing chests full of ribbons and gleaming Medals.
Suez, Aden, Gibraltar, Korea, Normandy, the Burma Star.
Veterans from every outpost, to the frontiers of the Empire.
A whole Industry to War and its aftermath, out on Parade!
Conscripts who gave their lives, and their families' in grief.
Inconsolable ~ Why the Hell were we fighting in Korea?
Some are left in the biggest war grave at sea, no relief.
Now he worries about a scratch on his car ~ A Mission.
The Salute taken by some pompous Duke, for Official recognition.
We're still tied up with Class and Role Models of Ego Superiority.
Your duty is but to do and die for King & Country or be a deserter.
"Who said, we've got to go to War?" Why? Must I die? For what?
A lost generation, cannon fodder; supremely Sacrificed just like me!
Whole War Industry; Armaments the biggest business in the World.
Killed for Nothing, the cost of a bullet, profitable for rich warmongers.
Stupid sop, only costs us £45 million a year for all this, Kow-towing!
Admiral of the fleet and Commanders in Chief, lining up all the ducks.
Where's our holy consort? Up on the balcony with a Rum and coke.
Must take them all morning to get their gold braid uniforms prepared.
The Prince of Wales' feathers; managed to lay them on the Cenotaph.
Why do the people put up with it? Patriots waving the Imperial flag.
Our Impoverished Pensioners today being pushed down Whitehall!
Princess Anne's got more Medals than my Grandad at Ypres.
She's never even seen a trench. A Rear Admiral of what mate?
Look at her Epaulets! Here comes the last Royal wreath layer.
On behalf of all Fascist representatives of the commonwealth!
And look at Tony the phony with his pack of wagging poodles!
Not a common welfare, dying, wounded in foreign, illegal wars!
Full Respect to You who did your sacred duty to end Fascism.
Did you discover, enlightenment as Arjuna on the battlefield?

33

<u>(being beingness)</u>
Never needing to interpret 'Le Chien Andalou' anymore.
Not being, 'Conditioned', 'Belle de Jour' Unconditioned.
Surreal Unconventionalism, cut it all or don't cut it all ~
Television and education and careers and relationships.
So called successes & failures; don't have to inform you,
how to live your life! You are living, your life is connected.
They don't have a clue of what it Is, It's beyond their limits
of what they are Conditioned to perceive it to be Taotally.
*

<u>Skunky monkey with a Solar flare</u>
Surrrealy * surreal that's never ending reconnections.
A whole lot of love in the Synapse's lounge.
Met a lot of eccentrics at the Class A….. Clinic
Closure, closure, closure ~
Go back and see (her) again.
There's nothing there for you.
A Rich gang of smack heads!
Always being fertile, by the Nile, don't dam that smile.
Experiencing Italian Chillums and chilies in their curries.
Those had horns on helmets, conventions of Barbarians!
Mixing all the Time, shape-shifting for Aristotelian answers ~
You come from the Earth Mother going to the Cosmic Mother
*

<u>The Free Press</u>
Inc.
*

<u>On this our *Jewel In the Sky</u>
Sweet surrender, sweet surrender ~ Out of Mind experience.
Does it make any sense, does it have to make any sense?
In Ibiza or was it Greece where we had our perfect moment.
Or were they psychedelic rainbows reflecting in your face ~

<u>My friend's favourite Cheech & Chong</u>
"don't come a knockin' if the van's a rockin"
If you got any Awareness of the drug, a Toker!
Stood Test of Time ~ barking at invisible Paranoias.
Such an hysterical sketch, so insanely funny.
I'm obviously going crackers.
Starting to like trance music…
But I was spoilt with great DJ's.
Third-eyeing on Psyche*activos, not in any Thesaurus!
What & how, ringing inside my head, can find it scary.
"Mind and body lose contact ~ Moon walking
Ketamine at the corner shop. No f…. thanks!
Laughing Buddha dissolving in a vat of Acid.
See if I can get hold of the girl ~
with telepathy on her hips
*

<u>Aiding Aids</u>
"No fuck is worth it!"
Shagsville, low will power ~
Going to bed with the Angel of death
Wings of a sociopathic bird on fire.
Painting of men's and angels'
Hysteria.
Krishna or man's mental speculation?
The Martians will run from Earth.
Not fit to live here
*

<u>Mumbai Hindu Urban Myth</u>
"They fuck goats in Afghanistan".
Things I've heard but never seen.
So is it true? I'm listening in on Your deep breathing ~
Patterns of a screamer not a dreamer ~ "Keeping it Real"
She's studying the neurological basis of Spirituality. Uhm!
"Left lobe processes info. ~ about ideas of Time & Space"

"Namaste"
"I'm honouring the Holy Spirit of me in Your reflection"
"You're honouring your Holy Spirit in My reflection"
Traditionally ~ don't get in my Personal Space!
Hand gestures, even the shadow of a Dalit ~
an Indian Untouchable, can cause discomfort!
You don't know about Racism in the west; yet!
*

All
Equally Poor!
'The Rich List' - of an Oligopoly
Fortune, 500 of 7.5 billion souls.
Six men own half the Planet's wealth!
*

Austerity Digitally
Council cutbacks with online sites. "Unavailable until…
further notice." No info. Your fault if you break the Law!
You got to pay, even to piss. No Public Conveniences
in a city of 15 Million. Perks, sucked her way to the top.
Real business will know all your weaknesses…
Sexual Axe: send in a whore, she'll get the top secret.
Pussy power & a cocaine monkey on your back; Smack!
Or your trip jumps into you. Have women lost the plot?
'Sexie, divorcee with a sweet, salty Yoni on offer'.
Cocaine rushin' through her demonic brain!
Sniff, sniff, wham, bam, thank you mamba.
Right in the middle of that, check all your dials…
*Chi from Prana Patterns * What is an Abstract Art*
Exhibition? Do I have to Know, should I know?
Have a Reiki wash, cleanse for Self-reference.
We're already in the Spaceship inside us ~
*Activation * Visualisation * Realign*
In an Illuminated egg

Ma Ganga.

"I'm a Chocaholic in Europe; ate 48 cream eggs in two hours"
Want to keep you in security, freaking out without a Mars bar.
Computers actually made people more stupid, Artificial Intel,
Cloned, Made to Order, Civilised, Conditioned Sheeple.Com.
Multi*dimensional /\\V/ with lascivious Lilith at Hill Top Party.
Deep feeling, Enjoying in Goa, keeping your wits about you.
How easy do you want it? Perfect, Please, a Natural Smile ~
Met a sister of Turquoise Pearl; Babaji came to visit Anjuna.
Lived in a Chillum Circle ~ build yourself up like a Volcano.
Good Day Out. The parties bring us together, spangled.
"A Certain amount of Paranoia keeps you safe mate"
Free pleasure, without lookin'; "Hallo I'm Zaratnustra"
Wearing a trance t-shirt: 'Goa * Friendly Healthy Abuser'
Throbbing Pudenda ~ what is that in Sanskrit or Swahili?
Always have a Metaphysical dictionary handy...
The people aren't dancing ~ the birds aren't trancing,
being submissive. Worshipping the mayhem of Shiva.
Stay in the essence ~ side-tracked inside a bird trap.
Be above it, flying like an eagle, gliding like a Swift ~
Let it go, let it flow, don't try to control it or it will control you.
"Work: when you live a divine life every day's a holiday."
Covered in blessings ~ in the land of the extinct Tiger!
*

Maybe it's all sat chit anand

Classic Asperger syndrome of the Sheriff. The reasons for sociopathic torturers!
Yes, he was trying to communicate and build bridges to find a solution, wasn't he?
There are others who are selling deadly weapons to extreme, misogynic, Royal-
Religious dictatorships. Is that the best we can do? It's like an insane Matrix!
Guruji having a laugh with an old illuminati tyrant, what's that all about?
Maybe he's also a ventriloquist? Maybe it's a true confession…
Knowing Liberation of Your Mind from your Mind ~ Unbound.

Need to Fly
That's what happens, MDMA. Bombay 2 am...
The Police have been arrested for not stopping
the Parties! Relax, shut my eyes, not give a shit.
She knows all the weirdoes and freaks
And She loves it...
Every shop's a coffee shop.
*
Internal Torture
You don't crawl, Up the wall......
Waiting for a Woodbine & Tequila to get you home
She's Live! Charas, treacle toffee...
Sitting there waiting for the drugs to come up.
Peaking on chai, hash biscuits & bhang liquors.
*
Pinpointing, 'A Police State'. Had it all in Chile!
Place of Zero Tolerance, No excuses for anyone...
Don't take it Personally, we are detaining your children...
Sending them for special Enhanced Interrogation techniques.
To your benign Dictators, House of Common assault on us..
Its Mind's hallucination ~ Happy and Healthy, be here now.
Driving you Mad, living down Snake alley ~
Crystal Meth. lying wasted, spaced out. Smack!
These are deadly, staying away from bad drugs.
*An Illusion * All delusion; go with it ~ Observe it.*
Playing with the visions; why be ~ scared of it?
Leap frogging around ~
*You become Super*Sonic.*
Through the phantasmagoria
** becomes a crystal clear trip **
Lots and lots of psychedelics.
Floating for two weeks ~ I Am!
FULL LOVE*

*In the music * in everyone*
*Waking up Inside You * Co-Creational Seeds.*
Bioneers ~ Biofeedback Prana Consciousness.
"the tree still grows" not in this Geo-warfare!
"The old always makes way for the new"
Refining torture methods, crypto eugenics.
Is life really too short? A Punch card, now
Breathe ~ and just see what happens…
'Dead Lines' > Up Shit Creek, Off-line!
DNA. Ego's bloody extension, brave, new
Planet. Everything they can do, Surprise!
Flowers fighting to survive, beyond ~
Now, we're all part of Cosmic Nature.
I didn't want to live by the Alarm, clock
Cock! Never by Time ~ In Enslavement.
Fished us in again and again, got you at it.
To keep us all busy, so we never ask, 'WTF; WHY?'
Blowing your Mind, smart, Artificial Intelligence Technology.
Electric Meters, we've been Made, to Pay, Obey, the Lord.
To believe we're going somewhere, doing what you're told!
Separated, right way or wrong way, don't know any more ~
That's what you get for inviting dark energy into the Unknown.
Only needs Fine Tuning inside ~ flying through the jet streams.
"The fuckin' dog took my sandals." She's got a new IBM. tattoo!
Love their servitude, "I've convinced myself, I have no pain.
Wife tying my shoe laces, I'm ever so sorry mate."
I'm being Shanti today, trying to make it my best friend.
"And I said to the Wife ~
At the time….
"All rivers flow to the Ocean"
You're multi-tasking, driving it on automatic.
"She asked me to knock her up, at 5am."
"It never rains but it f……g pours!"

Destroying Ignorance
"Acid breaks down all the systems & remakes them!"
It doesn't feel like that ~ it is that, feel it for yourself.
We have all the time in the world we have, Yin Yang.
Giving birth to an interior Milky way*Yes if you want.
Through the suffering you learn to pass the Mind by.
Realisations, destroying its false ego. Lord of 3rd eye ~
Takes away everything, throws it in the air ~ not a joke.
Blessing being ~ left within your own sense of self.
It was never only a concept of Identity, spinning it.
Vishnu's breathing In ~ Shiva breathing Out.
"Without Time ~ Space * doesn't exist." Babaji.
Nothing's there without Kali * Mother Nature *
La Creatrice, linking to your own supreme saviour.
Satguru, teacher gives you a technique to witness Spirit ~
but You have to link up Your*self * Your Inner Conscience.
No one is between You and Omnipresent Omniscience ~
Direct connection now to innate Origin ~Your higher Self
*

Time is Male ~ 'the Destroyer' nothing lasts
forever * 10,000 light years from a dead star.
Another dying Sun sucked into a black hole, baby.
Your Solar System disappears, reappears where?
It never broke the link, Yin*Yanging, Shiva*Shakti.
Time*Space*Time*Space*Time*Space*here*now ~
Time is one of Shiva's names, Kali is Space, bring it on!
*

She got married in a white veil!
Every track dedicated to every milligram…
On the 7th day Shiva created hashish, fill in the blanks.
"It's harder to turn your back on the drug dealer ~
than a friend." Seeing it through a Clear Lake.
"She's got a soft spot for the Phoenicians.
I don't conclude anything about past lives ~ fine.

The Evolution

Change the name of the Bible ~ Empire Jester Politics.
Having to Salute the cruel Invader, greedy Memsahib…
Converted hokum, hedonists, jet set, Maharaja playboys.
Feeding Global pressure, their Ignorant, Selfish pleasure.
Pirates they'd fill up their ship, got away with more looting!
Broke their own country; starvelings in their pillaged fields.
Paying highest taxes, jobless, desperate, ready for a War.
Kept on a boat, 'Shanghaied' 'Signed up', went exploring!
They employed Moslem butchers for a Holy Fatwah feast.
All slaughter houses belonged to them, killers of the Beast.
Not serving their people, only Imperial interests. Cf course..
"On the material reality, humans doing it better than animals!"
It's not about God creating the World in seven days, a week!
Who are You? A Creation Myth, some folks like killing humans.
Look, there's more love and compassion in the eyes of a cow!
Whose milk did you drink more of? They'll never be satisfied.
Trusting You not to feed them any Mad disease. Respectfully!
They didn't eat your mother or burn your sister and brother ~
Who's chosen the dark ~ Anti-time back to the Aryans, Whoa!
"Mahatma Gandhi is a fairy story; to some they think he's God"
No time for this shit dimension in an Astral Age ~
How to get back to the Mother ship …….

*

Syzygybot Question

Martian; sex with a green monkey,
they must be cute, the new hybrid,
the missing link & you wanna be ~
Sandalwood ash floating in the river
or in the ground, eaten by maggots?
Becoming worm shit ~ Black Magic Pan.
Captivating Power, enslaves, influences; Rights!
Fatwahs in your soup; married to an ex-Super model.
Territorial, Animal Jealousies that will cut your throat!

41

Artless Art
Diamond Cobras ~ got to get past the heart * Chakra.
Images, reflections, emotions, shining in the mirror image.
Diseased when you get identified with the negative ~ vibes,
thoughts ~ keeping us busy with the big, bogeyman bollocks.
As Programmed; It's Illegal to pick those Magical mushrooms.
FULL HAPPINESS
*

Wrong but Ok
You grow to like each other ~
'The Real Thing' ... A load off my Mind.
Never give up no matter what. Proper liquid..
"I'm an open book Baba". Diamond notes at night.
You've got the freedom, to do whatever you want.
A no lose situation; Muscovite, have one at your beck
and call for a week. Lost the Patriotic, neurotic, narcotic.
*

Again, the Universe doesn't Recognise Mind
Flying, is that just nerves? No it's Fear. Don't know
how you do it! Taking a deep breath all on my own.
No past Life, nothing. I can smell burnt wires, fine!
Is that an Open Mind or an explosive delusion?
What star? 'Praying Spirit' 'Om Shiva' > travelling ~
be happy & enjoy. I took another dimension through Peru.
Full on myth, unless it's a spectrum of an Incan Milky Way!
Super conscious asleep, Super conscious awake ~ presently
Super conscious Alive, channeled through Lakshmi's Bhakti.
I'm on many things right now, I cannot stay.
Black hole condensing colour in your cheeks,
many people are keeping up their frequency ~
looking to carry on, the lines of conscious energy.
26 degrees, Cosmic Opening into a double Taurus.
Jupiter's violet Space portal into realms of existence.
Astral Machu Pichu * Alignments with No Judgments.

Biometric Rivers

Going with the flow ~ Powers that be completely.
Undertows against the inner Amazone; exploitation!
Exploits - Lighthouse from the other side ~ all smiles.
The pain was so great, took me out of my Mind paradigm.
Out of my lifeboat, drowning, couldn't float ~ saw a vision.
Drifting tides, by a stream, beyond the reef into Surfers Bay.

*

Culture Dish

'Celebration of Ego' - Full Western Materialist's
Values ~ I'm always lookin' for the Magic.
Create your frequency to be Creative ~
Testing of evolution ~ expressions of energy.
Forged in a Star afar, we all share astral dust.
Pick up your lightning * we're goin' deep inside!
Into the dark matter, sparkling, shining bright,
with invisible energies to our human senses

Listening to the 'Addictions'

Sex on his Mind every 20 secs.
Never satisfied, in completeness.
Slave to a shaved pussy ~ purring within himself.
Went up like a flame thrower in a car.
Went up like a big ball of Fire!
Jumped into the wet concrete, he was lucky.
Found a jam tart fuckin' on trains…

*

Her Cowry

Shell of femininity ~ beautiful, attractive illusions.
Who nurtured and shared this lovely Gardenia?
African Aboriginals connecting Gondwanaland.
Designs from a Masai warrior wife's breasts.
Sacred lands inside of her ~
hearing songs of exotic birds

Bog of unnatural ingredients

Metal Bars on All the windows…
on a fully laden burning train ~ driving
through the desert; screaming for rain!
Got a feeling, opened up a clear channel.
Ego's mirages going into a lonely night ~
Alighting in terror, desperation and fright!
She's got off at the black hole terminal.
Changed to the Bhakti Super Express
Running through a field of white rabbits

*

Eros Cliché

You can shed some tears, let's bury the hatchet.
No such thing as bad publicity! Death to the Ego.
Shooting through the light doorway to Heaven.
No fear, no death, a mad genius!
It crossed the mind ~ and the reefs of delusion.
Holds you on track, psychic beams on your back.
The Art of Mindful or Mindless or neither; Yes Space.
Keep it Clear, Clean, Open, Fertility, Psyche*activity.
Ignorance stops release ~ becoming dispassionate.
"It's not that the Sun's gone anywhere ~
it's that the dark clouds have come over"
Freedom from ~ beings fully committed to change.
"New language speaks of a new design, art, patterns,
geometry, new vibrations ~ fully tuning, dancing lights

*

Rock Bottom * light to light * Sunwaves

In honour of the Sun * Sacred ~ Cosmic marriage.
Spiritual Union of Man & Woman, auras of equality ~
Clarity with a Sacred female, womb of the Goddess.
A split second devoid of thought ~ Nirvana Orgasms.
Blossoming, female genitalia, Orchid's beauty.
Made love with the most sublime, divine

My Life's Love
Companion's passing into mulberries.
The Temple of Revelation
Master of Imagination ~
Magic of the Sun
Source of all graces.
Spellbound before the pictures
of devoted, faithful Shepherdesses.
A beloved lady's Inspiration ~
New intrinsic conceptions.
Working with their heads
Gathering living Secrets
Noblesse of Spirit

*

Sorcerer's flight
Surreal world talking in Psytrance beats.
Always ask Yourself, who you really are?
Keep it simple and easy ~ delight…
Understanding with Full Compassion
Forgiveness that gets rid of doubt and guilt.
"It's forgiveness from the heart ~
that gets rid of guilt from the heart"
Living with a poet, naked, down by the sea.

*

La belle nature
Le garcon aux yeux gris ~
et une des plus belles filles de France.
"You're the first to come back, can I ask why you left?
Sharing a secret in love, under pastel, pink cherry trees.
Whispering in your eyes
Answers to a wonder ~
"I want to be with you, forever"
Can you tell me how you feel?
Distractions, talking to herself

The Turtle
"Once extinct you will only be able to Imagine it"
The Imagination; every day is a natural blessing.
it's gone forever, You'll find their galactic trail ~
She's going to try and civilise him. Good luck.
They come from two different dimensions…
Killed in an air raid in Amiens!
Freaking out; "got a cigarette?"
Don't lose your temper, hold your breath, for how
long darling? But don't lose your short term memory ~
"This place is so peaceful, never know there was a War!"
"She's acting odd, isn't she?" "Pas spécialement"
*

Togetherness
Perceiving In-Sanity as Shanti.
"Even prostitutes have feelings"
Direct experience, got it firsthand.
Yes, let's use the acrimonious pain to see a light come on,
might realise what the rest of us went through! Empathy.
Returning to the roots not Adversarial madness darling.
Vile legal system got it all wrong on purpose, dangerous.
Obvious corruption and ignorance plus possessive greed.
State sponsored terror. Let's have the truth for our children
*

"Who Am I, Where do I come from, Where am I going?"
Choose ~ a Muse not a corporate, Fake News Channel.
*High lights * High frequency ~ long, tall, high thighs.*
Streaming Free energy ~ light through your open heart.
She really sticks her claws in you and holds on tight!
Up, no demons, deep emotion, reflecting colored mirrors.
'Rebel'- don't label Yourself, don't label Myself, Is liberty.
Real Time Astronauts traveling through the Light barrier.
Instigate, Full Beam Consciousness ~

Conception of a Mystical Poet
Spirit is something bigger than Your Self, a name.
Standing at the graveside, standing by the flame.
Family and friends in shock, loss, sadness, grief!
Gone back into our Cosmos, dropped the body off.
Your Time is Your Celebration of boundless infinity
Inside You & Me, scattered on the elemental winds.
Memories of a lifetime so sweet, so sublime darling.
Never what one expects

*

I Am ~ As It Is
All in the Eyes ~><~ the Spirit of Russia.*
Crawling out the flames of a razed heart.
The memories of unimaginable, cruel reality.
Terror rising, more Innocent victims in Abattoirs.
Strangling the tenderest hearts of Cosmic starlets
that once kissed you in Spring, beside a river's meadow.
"They paid a high price for freedom, 20,000,000 killed!"
Walking through an horrifically mutilated deathscape

*

Jesus Is Not for Eugenics
Left a full lunatic asylum, cock a doodle do.
Now ~ what are you; God knows!
Do you like what you see?
Reflections in the Sunshine.
Everything is dictated to you by the Mind.
Cold and expensive, "I don't speak English".
In the kitchen boiling dumplings.
Took the Metro from Sumperfopol to Moscow.
Humanity at the edge of something happening ~
Challenge to Individual Identity, Mass conformity,
Cloning, genetic manipulation, Security, Control Command.
What do you believe and know of reality ~ when separated

Kailash Air
"Just following the path all the way to China;
You need a special guide." Cold hungry nights...
Legends & roots of Paradise on Earth ~ Shangri-La.
Markets of a ruined city with frankincense and Myrrh.
She passed the Shrine of Vishnu the Preserver.
If you answer with a True heart ~
took him to the Crystal Mountain,
there they first made love within a sacred landscape.
Shiva & Parfait Parvati's honeymoon, ethereal dawn.
Lake Manasovra ~ Centre of this Planet of the Mind.
Different conceptions of Time & Space ~ in existence.
Hidden in stupendous valleys at the End of the World.
Met the serene Consciousness of a Grand Magician.
She'd joined a caravan of Yak herders to Shambala.
Prophecies of Padma, found in the ancient Sutras.
Led an expedition to discover the source of the Ganges

*

Peas
Going through
A Process ~
Processing
Processed...
& fresh fig juice
Poetical not geometrical.
Not Violating fundamental principles
of rare, green Iridescent spiders ~

*

Characteristic Attractions.
Ubiquitous, Carrot & Stick ~ no victims live here; Really!
Self-Indulgent, Mind wandering, daydreaming, Bi-Polars.
Found I had dyspraxia, she had glorious, OCD. ADHD.
Married in a Cathedral where they'd butchered Cathars.
White Lights of Consciousness, glowing in your promise...

<u>"I'm on two phones here"</u>
So L.A. * "Yeah, Buy, Sell it All!"
I'll meet her out there, we'll Rage, rampage!
Smell the cookin' ~ I don't want to handle it...
Brainwashed by Magnetism along Sunset Strip.
The Hypnotic approach, Charismatic suggestions.
A Phoenician beauty gave me a drink of Foxglove ~
appearances of hallucinations, at the Circus Maximus.
Once an Oracle in a Pagan Temple.
Offering thrills and spills….
*

<u>Prayer flags & Secret Tests</u>
"Patriotism is the last refuge of Scoundrels"
Disgusting grenade launchers, Pre-Genghis Khan.
Stuck with a horror behind a razor wired warrior!
This is a Power Station living In Mind Expansion.
Cloning Stealth Bombers to end our World.
Witness of a Waitress in a Madhouse.
Unknown fear, back then in the village.
On a country steam train to beyond Udipi ~
energies of the land, contaminated for centuries!
Forcing more Maya out near Laxmanjhulla bridge.
The Salvation Army made lovely cups of tea.
The shot at dawn, got a Posthumous pardon
from the Pigeon Association…
*

<u>Faithfully ~ Fell from Pagan Pleiades</u>
"It's a lot for a liver to take." Atom Bomb on Fire,
or Marilyn Monroe cavorting with Coke bottles!
Balls of Light * Battleships in a Sky of hungry Comets.
Goa ~ gives me something to dream about! For how long?
Munchies, I must be the luckiest guy in the world.
Goa, "Definitely * maybe ~"

<u>Don Quixote Vision of a Marvelous Impulse</u>
Always Keep high, no abusing if using ~
Boggling the Mind, its logical boundaries.
Boggling the Crown Chakra
My entry into Venus' waters
through your Universal Yoni.
My entry into the nature through high Spirit.
My entry to the Cosmos, through thy 3rd eye.
Surprise interstellar sunrise ~ Mind's Concept.
Getting so close up, keep it sweet, lustful Satyr.
From the sublime depths of Aphrodite's magical grotto.
She is Ultra-Creatrice, arrived on a plane from Moscow.
"Never use Programmed words as has been said before,
& no more psychological manipulations or power games!
Let the Inspiration keep your spirit free and loving ~
dissolving moulds, realising the intentions, feeling Space.
The inner Love, Heart calling, found what I was looking for ~
synchronically tuned into the Ocean's morning, gentle breeze
In your hair, in your mouth ~
every moment
*

"My Universe your Uterus, there is no mould in reality".
*You put yourself on All the Spaceships ~ in Time*sense.*
She'll kick the door down to get free, you know how it is!
"I know who trances and I know who dances Baba"
All of Life is a Meditation, sharing a lot of Infinity ~
Pachamama lets it grow, nature's crystal snow, be clear.
Is there too much going on in your Mind, had no Idea!
Did you see Gopis loving Krishna? I'll take your word for it.
With the US. cavalry out on Location, where are they now ~
Camp Euphrates with gruesome, bloody red, Little Bighorns.
Drop the Imagery ~ "My Heart Is Broken"
Reflecting it back onto Itself

50

Inattentive Coercion

All the Social diseases, poverty, corruption, violence, War,
exploitation, bullying, illiteracy, propaganda, Separation,
Ignorance, greed, envy, jealousy, domination, cruelty,
intolerance, religious inquisition, torture, obsessions,
Addictions, persecutions, lying, stealing, guilt, sin. Etc.
The News makes us depressed, needs to take tranquillizers.
Legal/illegal drugs to take away the pain, blame, shame, grief.
On the autistic spectrum, is known to have shown symptoms,
neurodiverse disorders, prone to panic attacks, secret tests!
ADHD. your short term memory, you forgot I am your Lover.
Daydreaming you fell for 'coup de foudre'. Obsessional to a point.
You denied my very existence, rejected my caresses, physically,
your muscles are divine but you wouldn't let yourself be touched.
"How does your Motor function, Baby?" Brain thinking too much,
then a complete Shutdown, another of your bipolar syndromes.
'Specific development disorder' strange spatial ~ perceptions, do
you know that I am here sharing your life; still loving a sociopath?
Or were you Misdiagnosed with fatigue, means virus or a crisis?
Your frustration and low self-esteem for our couple, what does it
mean; can it also be a blessing, gift? Repression and regression,
my concubine's problem, 'sensory Integration dysfunction'.
Her over sensitivity to touch, can't be loving too much.
Fear, it took her to a 'Borderline personality disorder'.
You left me, with 'Emotional dysregulation' ~ Visualisation.
Took your mood swings, hysteria & delirium, gave em to another
to recover. We disconnected and made a 'hyper-derealisation'.
Didn't feel the outburst, aggression would affect me so strongly.
How to be aware of so much sensory information darling and be
so in love with you! I met a sexy cavalier, normal interactions until
she took a poison of denial. 'Somaform disorder' on her nerves ~
The pain was Real!

Surreal Ocean
Kind for kind, on the lake of your Mind.
More than the dance to the Supreme ~
If you crash your car you get a new one.
Got a different one here. You had it (death) not rebirth.
'Atman' just words, it is there; 'Soul' is just there too!
The Mind blowing * bubbles ~ isn't it all a mirage?
Just to survive here now you have to be spiritual!
Prophets everywhere, gorgeous, 'No Woman No Cry'.
Reality mish mash, planetary, shanti Bodhisattvette
on the way to a jungle beach, under a Banyan tree.
Flew in on a spiral of Love, kept her in reach ~
Cooing, besotted dove, Spirit of Cupid in the air.
Vedic mathematics, Quantum dematerialising
passed the door, walked through the walls ~
dropping out using 5 elements & Vishnu's wife.
Lakshmi's blessing, abundance has everything
_*_

Build a church, Open a business for sinners.
Vedanta - men free of desires, but tempted!
Unnatural, only Shiva can give rebirth ~
Formlessness can take any form that's given to us.
_*_

Saraswati - needing wisdom with the wealth.
"That money will not stay" ~ forever on horizontal time?
Osho's enlightened energy, everything is coming to him.
They gave Socrates hemlock, or he gave it to himself?
All rivers flow into the Ocean
Then there's no rivers ~ effect and reaction.
"Christ Consciousness is not Christian
It's Cosmic ~ You reap what You sow."
_*_

"Patriotism is serving your country all the time
and your Government sometime." Mark Twain.

Deception * Perception

'The lesser of two evils is still evil', the hidden, sleight of hand.
'You know what, being called Mad by an Idiot Is a complement'
David Icke's clarification of another Proxy war, the back story.
'Demonising Russia to go to war with them, yet they are still
supporting racist Zionism, evil Saudi Arabia, bombing Yemen!'
Who's selling them all these Weapons for Mass Destruction?
Seeing the blatant contradictions, time to wake up Major Tom!
'The Human race has given up its power to Mad, Psychopaths.'
Who broke the Bank of England, devaluated people's savings?
Any members of the Club of the Isles, Quantum Hedge Funds?
'War is Peace, Freedom is Slavery, Ignorance is Strength'
'They stole their Olive groves and blocked the water wells.'
Dark forces financing the Slave trade, started Opium wars!
"What do you think will happen granddad?"

*

Synergetic Shiva

If I'm gonna have it ~ You're gonna have it.
That's the way it is ~ chill*om

*

Risk of a Flight Fuck

Trusted her every time ~
She betrayed me every time...
She really fucked me every time too!
My super sexy, X generation Dhammayanti.
And Judas hung himself from the nearest tree.
Juliet took poison for her everlasting, dying Love
and so did her Romeo; "Eros I know how you think."
"Do you think you know how my mind thinks?" "I think so"
Sita protected her purity yet was led into the fire of Sati!
'It is now illegal to have sex with your underage, virgin wife!'
You impose nothing and give a lot of friendly encouragement.

Unfuckin' believable Ectogenesis
Birthing a baby in a plastic grow bag!
How about a trip to Amsterdam Baba?
He went into the other room to die ~
"I never thought it would be like this,
but it's brilliant, no fear, part of nature."
'Life coming to the end as the passing of the day'
Naively took too much Acid Punch for the trance.
Going to the next party at Curlies & Shiva's Valley.
Fantasies, It's not your morality, you're just dancin'
Believing in it all doesn't matter where it goes ~
Following ~ I am here now

*

Go Ahead Go Ahead, At All Times
'Mano a mano', leveraged ~ met peyote Don Juan!
"Don't want to deal with someone with nothing to lose.
Heart & Soul of American people carrying guns in their car,
"A Yankee is an enemy to anyone from the South"
Grunts, "You're either with us or against us Mentality"
They excel at it, Psycho-path of a Robot-Rumsfield Profiler.
Breaks you down and Rebuilds you in their own Image!
Boys from the South loved it couldn't get enough of it...
"Ready to Roll, kill those fuckers!"

*

Red, Blue and White Gestapo!
Rewriting the Rules of Engagement Book.
Lied to the Whole World on Prime Time TV.
Can't sell it - Another Massacre to the Public. Heil!
'Invading is Liberating', their Gold! Give me a break!
All about Plunder (& Enhanced Stress Techniques!)
Hand in Hand ~ They Vote with a Shotgun in Dixie...
Fuhrer Bush campaigns in rattlesnake, cowboy boots.

Don't forget that Mental Margueritta.
Times up ~ "I'm livin' it"
'The drop outs' -'Better to have been free,
and lost, than never to have ~ been free '
I wouldn't go that far, I can see….
Spawn of Satan on your bathroom wall.
We've hit a nerve - that's how it should be.
We're fucked up; 'the Truth can hurt a lot!'
Games, 'Your arse is Big', It is what it is...
Reality Check, "want a baby?"
Little things can set you off - I Survived well here.
Without Sociopathic, horrible denial, Selfishness.
Fixation to having a baby, without you; thanks!
Hit another nerve, woke up a Chameleon, sister.
Russian beauty pulled me out of its hungry mouth.
Addiction you can't Control, never Mind Recognise;
If Your Mind and Heart are Obsessed, certainly can't!
Speaking tree, kill that fly! Programmed, Redialed, Filed.
But I have options, can't make my Mind up, in the process of..
Who said you could anyway; Ain't that easy!
"I AM A SUPER FAST PROCESSOR
WITH AN X X' EGO CHIP PROGRAM"
Going with the Free Flow < Real eyes >
I CAN'T EXPLAIN IT ~ Do I really need to …

*

Grasses
Takes you out of Your self
Smoking the Peace Pipe in a circle ~
Politician, You're a badmouth for Hire, full of lies'
Did you ever read, 'Legends and Myths of Hawaii'
by Chief KalaKaua, see what happened to them! But…
It's not for the good of the people. Saying anything to sell!
Brain dead Sheep; Neurological energy in another realm.
Responding to the Medulla Oblongata ~ How I live my life.

Organic/symptomatic: Dementia (Alzheimer's disease, Multi-infarct dementia, Pick's disease, Creutzfeldt-Jakob disease, Huntington's disease, Parkinson's disease, AIDS dementia complex, Delirium, Post-concussion syndrome, Psychoactive substance: Intoxication (Drunkenness) - Physical dependence (Alcohol dependence, Opioid dependency) withdrawal (Benzodiazepine withdrawal, Delirium tremens) Amnesic (Korsakoff's syndrome) Schizophrenia, schizotypal, delusional: Schizophrenia (Disorganized schizophrenia), Schizotypal personality disorder Delusional disorder, Folie à deux - Schizoaffective disorder. Mood: (affective) Mania, Bipolar disorder, Clinical depression Cyclothymia, Dysthymia Neurotic, stress-related & somatoform: Agoraphobia Anxiety disorder, Panic disorder, Generalized anxiety disorder, Social Anxiety Disorder, OCD, Acute stress reaction, PTSD. Adjustment disorder, Conversion disorder, Somatoform disorder, Somatization disorder, Neurasthenia Physiological/physical Behavioural: Eating disorder (Anorexia nervosa, Bulimia nervosa) Sleep disorder (Dyssomnia, Insomnia, Hypersomnia, Parasomnia, Night terror, Nightmare) - Sexual dysfunction (Erectile dysfunction, Premature ejaculation Vaginismus Dyspareunia persexuality, Postpartum depression. Adult personality & behavior: Personality disorder - Passive-aggressive behavior, Kleptomania, Voyeurism, Trichotillomania, Factitious disorder, Munchausen syndrome. Mental retardation. Psychological development disorder: Specific: speech and language (Expressive language disorder, Aphasia, Expressive aphasia, Receptive aphasia, Landau-Kleffner syndrome, Lisp) scholastic skills (Dyslexia, Dysgraphia, Gerstmann syndrome) motor function (Developmental Dyspraxia) Pervasive: Autism, Rett syndrome, Asperger syndrome Behavioural & emotional, childhood & adolescence onset: ADHD, Conduct disorder Oppositional defiant disorder, Separation anxiety disorder, Selective mutism reactive attachment disorder, Tic disorder, Tourette's

Symptoms and Signs (R00-R69, 780-789) - Wikipedia
Circulatory and respiratory systems: Tachycardia-Bradycardia-Palpitation -Heart murmur -Nosebleed -Hemoptysis, Cough, abnormalities of breathing (Dyspnea, Orthopnea, Stridor, Wheeze, Cheyne-Stokes respiration, Hyperventilation, Mouth breathing, Hiccup) -Chest pain -Asphyxia -Pleurisy -Respiratory arrest -Sputum -Bruit. Digestive system and abdomen Abdominal pain -Acute abdomen -Nausea -Vomiting -Heartburn -Dysphagia-Flatulence -Burping -Fecal incontinence -Encopresis -Hepatomegaly Splenomegaly -Hepatosplenomegaly -Jaundice -Ascites -Fecal occult blood -Halitosis. Skin and subcutaneous tissue: disturbances of skin sensation (Hypoesthesia, Paresthesia, Hyperesthesia) Rash, Cyanosis-Pallor -Flushing -Petechia -Desquamation -Induration. Nervous and musculoskeletal systems: abnormal involuntary movements (Tremor, Spasm, Fasciculation, Athetosis) - Gait abnormality lack of coordination (Ataxia, Dysmetria, Dysdiadochokinesia, Hypotonia) -Tetany - Meningism - Hyperreflexia Urinary system: Dysuria -Vesical tenesmus-Urinary incontinence - Urinary retention - Oliguria -Polyuria-Nocturia. Cognition, perception, emotional state and behavior: Anxiety, Somnolence, Coma, Amnesia (Anterograde amnesia, Retrograde amnesia) -Dizziness -smell and taste (Anosmia, Ageusia, Parosmia, Parageusia). Speech and voice: speech disturbances (Dysphasia, Aphasia, Dysarthria) -symbolic dysfunctions (Dyslexia, Alexia, Agnosia, Apraxia, Acalculia, Agraphia) - voice disturbances (Dysphonia, Aphonia) General symptoms and signs: Fever (Hyperpyrexia) Headache, Chronic pain, Malaise, Fatigue, Fainting, Febrile seizure -Shock (Cardiogenic shock) - Edema (Peripheral edema, Anasarca) Hyperhidrosis (Sleep hyperhidrosis) Delayed milestone, Failure to thrive, food and fluid intake (Anorexia, Polydipsia, Polyphagia) Cachexia -Xerostomia -Clubbing

Chakras' Hip Hop >:<Universal detachment
We'll make it go round ~ and round & ~
You are part of the creative mystic eye
Open the box of spirals
It's not possible, the Finite Mind to know the Infinite.
'Chilling Goddess'
I'm not an addict 'cause I can stop when I want! Wow!
Giving birth to a galaxy, destroying the false ego ~
*it's not a joke, Kali * Space doesn't really exist.*
The whole world runs on Time ~ It's there, God's Ego.
*Waste of time, better to realise who you are, here*now.*
*

A New Fatwa -This is not something Spirit wants
For the far enemy he recites a poem about Jihad
at his son's wedding. Insane as he's not Krishna!
We want to drag them into a War
Show the US as Infidel invaders, Invite their drones.
On a Martyrdom mission enrolling in a flying school.
Waving the Pirate flag, Yes, Recognising the brand!
Cutting off the head of the snake ~ Giant Anacondas.
America worships money, Al Qaeda now in franchise.
All you need is an idea and a laptop from Ikea…
Global Jihad, Another Global, Oligarch-Terrorism concept!
Blew up Tora Bora Mtns; another Stealthy, deadly mission.
Woke up to the Unexpected gift of a B52, US. invasion again!
Revival of revenge, another UN. Poodle -Territorial Imperative.
The Colin Powell Nexus; well what did you expect General?
*

Alchemical elemental
Everything affects you ~ a family man.
"Can't open any file without his identity!"
'Act of Invoking the Angel'
To this Jewel in the Sky

Shanti Art
Teddy bear given to the child.
When 'Separated' from its Parents. By Mad decree!
The decision was made, another sister went bonkers.
An advert for a Mental institution like a 5* resort. Yeah!
But she wouldn't want to go there.
You don't want to see the Gestapo in the street!
Met another man who was 'gaga....
let's take joy to the deserted Island
in the middle of a river,
full of wild ganga ~
white crystallite sand.
All the decisions were made by the Inner Circle.
Then I went insane & understood the Mind-game.
Thank your lucky stars tribal sister
*

Loyalty to the Clan of Fake Mass-Media
Hera Centaur, Medicine's 1st practitioner.
Myths express the Mind,
Sacred laws of hospitality.
Zeus, king of Powerful Ancient Gods ~
From a land few humans had ever seen.
Come to a psychedelic picnic at Magic Oak wood.
On the main caravan road crossing the Caucuses ~
Bitter, bloody feuds carried on for generations.
There they murdered all their men and their women!
Loving the riches, bling; law of the darkest jungles.
Back to the time of iron age, Invazion, Colonization.
Bands of Baron robbers; conflicts of good and evil.
And facing up to death ~ no such thing, Inshallah!
An alien land ruled by a very cruel Monster king.
Rules: Never show fear, don't look me in the eye.
Never look at the feminine with poisoned dreams

Obama Nation of Desolation
Worshipping the Black Cube of Satan.
'God said let there be light and there was...
Archonic broods of Vipers coming up from Hell.
'Abominations in the Temple, synagogue of Saturn'.
Chief exorcist says, 'the Devil is living In the Vatican'.
The Council of 33, Illuminati Power in the heart of US.
Believe in yourself ~ in the light Spirit of divine wo/man
*

In the Mecca of America
Secret societies, Freemason's Rites, Sociopathic elites,
International Eastern Star, Pentagrams, Satan's Pattern.
From ancient Egyptian to the Roman God of Time worship,
Set of evil, war, dark forces, chaos, devastation and hellfire!
Coming from the Tabernacle of Rephan, Moloch, Baal, Baphomet,
Horned Cernunnos, the Wicked Man, sorcery on a Globalised scale.
Ask Elijah, Ezekiel 8 v9, look in the Bible, Kabbalah, Revelations 3 v9.
All are profanities filled with the blood of innocents, burning your children.
Sacrificing your sons and daughters as offerings, in a room of false Idols!
Violence, 'They profess to know God but their deeds deny him'. Titus 1 v16.
They are the sons of destruction and lawlessness, the Antichrist revealed.
Where is the Spirit ~ in the hearts of wo*men co*existing in joyful peace?
*

It's easy to say, "I Forgive"
but we have to eliminate the seeds of pain, loss, betrayal, distrust,
resentment, anger, grief, attachment, despair, disillusionment, loss
of self-confidence that still exist in the sub-conscious, especially if
you've been in Love. How to eliminate these deep energetic fields
of suffering? It takes time and a conscious belief that the truth
will transcend and the hate and Ignorance will be dissolved.
'Hate dissolves with Love not more hate' ~ Dhammapada.

>>*Trans*mission* >>

Krishna says all things are from boundless Brahman.
'Can't describe the essence of the eternal Tao'. Simply ~
An Intuitively felt experience ~ words can transmit the idea'
"Golden, Holy Temples are unnecessary with Telepathy"
"When the Parietal lobe shuts down we can no longer
distinguish between our self and the rest of the World;
Subject believes, in tune with the timeless, infinite power."
'Feeling Spiritual experience ~ just a neurological illusion!
Temporal lobe area for language and conceptual thinking'
'God Lives in the Brain'…. so they said.

*

Japanese Orchid

different phenomena in the conditioned Mind,
not a neon Nazi CCTV. barking instructions.
The Last word on her tortured lips ~ "Liberté!"
She'd once written a book of '20 Jataka Tales'.
Later we lost the Aral Sea; we lost you and me.
"Nature ~ the ultimate Source not a Resource."
Spirits in the water, Spirits in the trees, alive.
Count Your blessings Chancellor.
Fine tuning butterflies

*

Jawohl Rules

Council Tax paying for a 'Zero Tolerance' Police State.
Very nasty, 'Final Notice', letters in red print, if you're late.
A heightened Sense of Appreciation when it all goes right!
DNA. evidence and fingerprints of teenagers being teenagers.
Keeping it on record, a meta-data file, for the rest of their lives.
If it ain't equal it ain't fair and that's no good.
It'll grind you up sooner or later ~
It's good we all share together
Streaming

The Crux of Extra-terrestrials
When you're living without Attachments
You got more Personal Freedom.
Existential ~ Multi*Dimensions

*

Is there such a thing as 'Holy War' at the intrinsic, infinity of existence?
The Bhagavad Gita suggests there is, as does Islam, Christianity and other ~
religions (Buddhism, Tao, Zen being accepted as philosophies). Jesus certainly
never professed War or ANY Violence in fact the sages profess Peace and Love.
And Jesus was the son of God! Gautama the Buddha taught the same; Loving
Kindness to all for good Karma and to end suffering. Why is the World full of death
and devastation especially on the innocents? Who gains from this loss and Pain?

*

Fascist Raper of the Sabines
The new Holy Plenipotentate; Blair to scare our children. Sieg heil!
Mr. War Bush, other insane criminals for Crimes Against Humanity!
What an epitaph and for your crones Messrs. Cheney, Rumsfeld?
Another Sociopath, Genocidal Monster; what else can you call it?
Got a front row Box at the Coliseum; throw in another Christian!
And we don't fuck around, this is the Kali Yuga we're in!

*

Orchestral Nature
'Life is simple, sharing Loving Kindness, from the heart'
I felt it in my Guru's metta ~ in tune with Love's full moon.
Going over limits, sailing over the edge, a line of Space time.
I don't know how to talk to you; Nature's flowers are singing.
Everyone else is busy focused on making more, more money.
Simply Amazing and he just can't roll a very good joint!
Do I give a fuck? Sat chit anand…
How do you express the Cosmic?
Being free of what exactly?

Idea
I want to be ~
An Angel
behave as an Angel
'Green Eve'
*

Turquoise Angel from Venus
Swam out of the reef of grief
Swam off Paranoia Island ~
Swam through coral shoals of Gold
*by way of a Psylocibin * Satyricon.*
Crystals all around, higher, higher!
Volition Not Violation
Do what you can
Character
*

Lilith's Afternoon (5,700,000 entries)
They found her beside the Red Sea ~
not so caught up in the straight net, Mind-set.
Less obsession, that's why we can chill more.
Magical fish predestined in their genetic DNA.
Deep blue Spirituality relaxing in the sunlit bay.
All natural Integration ~
Let go of the Black hole
of the Mind, limited-Mind.
Ego rocking ~ bhakti flowing
Rainbows of lovely, translucent lights ...
Beams in jungle groves of white Elephants.
Seen only by those with a pure vibrational heart.
They say Queen Maya conceived by Lake Anotatta ~
Life by the summer abode of swans; wise, sacred birds.
And Krishna tried everything to halt the Kurukshetra War!
7 survivors from the Pandavas and 3 from the Kauravas.
18 days, 4 million dead, many widows; began Kali's Yuga!

Met on the Lakshadweep Express
You can't figure it out
It's too Big ~ that's the Mind!
Pulling you in again and again.
Let it be, renewal ~Total Rebirthing
Opal Phoenixes rising from the ashes.
Maybe you got to be pretty simple.
All comin' through, all being true…
Revolutionary ~ of living in that vibe.
That's it, that's the One
In India travelling on the train to Goa ~
in a soft, cool, perfumed, night breeze.
Nature created it through their Minds,
it didn't just come in…
Shining through the window
*

Wizard Island or Rue Des Dames
'Manasarovar' ~ Sanskrit: 'Lake of the Mind'
Came from a source of the Brahmaputra & Indus.
Sitting beside the highest fresh water in the World.
To practice 'Dyhana' ~ Meditation in Crater Lake.
Death of the Ego, shooting into the Cosmic light.
Doorway to Heaven, no fear, no death or birth illusions.
Concentration (of the Mind), empty (Mind), clear (Mind).
Mad Genius on the seashore, playing an emerald conch.
Best fuck of our lives, under a radioactive, burning Sun.
*

Boxer for a Dollar
A dog called Shiva in a collar…
A snake in the XXXX Porno Suite.
Just sharing in the metta auras that's all there is.
Can we surrender to cancer and let it pass through energetically?
Can we pass through Universal spectrums with our Oyster card?

THE MAGIC

They are obviously psychopaths living in a Sociopathic, powerful
society, satiated by drinking the life force of the rest of us, if we allow it.
There are all those in the other parts of the blue sapphire, golden Topaz,
rainbow constellation, spectrum and those floating on sparkling, crystal crowns
surrounded by angels of light and magicians sitting on a thousand petal Lotus *
It is beyond my comprehension how humans can inflict such cruelty and horror
on other innocent people and on the infinity of natural, biological species in this
Celestial song ~ multi*dimensional * conscious feeling*dreamtime * Cosmos
Fascinating the hearts and imaginations of Lovers
*

I AM

NOT MY MEMORY * OR MY IMAGINATION

'Judge us not for our weakness but for our Love'
'The People we were fighting decided to fight back!'
In Present ~ 'Finite is here so the Infinite can be felt'
'My stamp came off in the sweat!'
BE IN G *HU MAN* BE IN G
Is this Paradise ~ of course
*

From Alien Frequencies

HARPPE can steer the Jetstream ~
Another Geo-weaponised system for War!
Cause a drought, cause a storm, dust bowls.
Left their land for a better future, not fracking.
Building a monster from Nature under your home.
Your Government's poisoning our ground water supply.
"Control the water, you control the people!" Thanks Your Highness.
Death, Destruction, devastation, Agenda 21, surveillance, 24/7 in my box.
Keeps rain away, Conglomerates sucking up each drop, killing your village!
Le clochard Celest is asking, who the fuck are these Archon-hybrids mate?

Bufo toad's gift of slimy foam
"I met my frog
I never expected to meet my frog.
He didn't even jump ~
Drugs from the Jaguar frog people,
You are the Sky"
You're going through the Matrix >Creation
If you can Activate your brain ~
*You're Krishna * man*
Transcending the grey matter.
The walking upright Man came…
The Plant Queen Is to remind you
of how amazingly beautiful you are.
Connecting with the Higher Self, a Star.
Dream world ~ Other stuff was happening.
Earth Rise, 1st Peek of (Outer) Earth from Inner Space.
More outgoing, infrared, trapped in hotter atmosphere.
*Chemtrails * CO2 carbon dioxide, greenhouse gases.*
40% of Population's getting water from the Himalayas.
Soil evaporation with heat ~ no more Time to compete!
*

*Pale Blue Limbic * "Am I still rich?"*
That's the future in which we're going to live our life ~
Why didn't you wake up? Seduced by sparkling auras.
Priapic, Ironic, Moronic, Dystopic, Platonic, Utopic.
Projector ~ I can see the light behind the screen.
Travelling young and able without worrying…
about the money, enjoy the great experience!
** Older and able is cool too * inside * outside **
*Quantum speed * Aller Retour * Venus.*
Chiaroscuro Goddess' Light Magic

Dead Sunbeam

The Sahara was once the African fertile, Ma Amazonia.
Last Ice Age 11,000 years ago. Wow, what do I know!
Arctic floating Ice Poles, Perma-frosting ~ melting floes.
In 50 -70 years, No Ice caps, keeping Earth Chilled out!
Oceans get hotter as it melts; more flooding, rain falling.
Planetary Engine redistributing heat, effects air currents.
Gulf Streaming, more salt, denser, colder currents sink ~
Lizards in a (burning) bush ~ expiration of Orang u tans!

*

Katrina's wakeup call at the 17th street canal. WMD…
Weather of Mass Destruction. "Please come this way!"
Melting Greenland, bye-bye Florida, au revoir Brussels.
2 billion Chinese coal polluters, 8 billion on the horizon.
Natural resources, forest fires burning, forever and ever ~
We're Mindlessly continuing the Dinosaur habits of the past.
Days of reckoning, Bang! Bedevil our thinking, in oblivion.
Misconceptions deliberately learned; a gas lobby tortoise.
Can't face the facts, only sees reality as obstacles, risk, fear!
Their insane understanding, their Identifying, their conditioning.
Our choices in our hands; 0.001% Illuminati on 1st extinction list.

*

Circus Maximus

Offered thrills and spills
by a sultry, Cathagian beauty Queen.
Morning glories in her sweet, perfumed hair.
Once an Oracle in a Pagan, fertility Temple ~
Carrying off a long legged Sabine in his arms!
Pan-Sexual, holographic, Book of Beginnings.
The Gatekeepers ~ "Friend or Foe?"
It crossed my Mind ~
Massive amounts of LSD.
They're already here…

Depends what or who you know or don't know.
The nude restaurant I had a nervous breakdown in.
Met her there, a blonde, Lee Strasberg movie star.
Painting dollar bills, relaxing with a ripe banana;
came with Avant Garde, Dada, Taomato soup.
A Savant… Teaching us to be free ~ 'It's easy!'
Breaking the Supra-Conditioning of 'Identifiction'
of Self. One more 'Giant leapfrog for mankind'.
A Miracle any survived, still shimmering, aglow!
Jewels cascading out of her beautiful, long hair.
*

Hand Outs & Missed Bargains
He loved making people beg for money!
Emerald diamond bracelets for Lily Love.
Pure Abstract Expressionism ~ of course
*

A Visual Pop Stencil
"If you don't use it > you lose it"
Open Mind ~ True to Your Inner Self.
Positive Risk > Realising, Obsessive Addictions.
*A Rocky Star * Crack, cracking, cracked smart tar.*
St. Vitrius' dance of holy cats from out of darkest Africa.
An Artist's eye for physical beauty arousing Sexual appeal.
Twirling Fire dancers discovered on hidden Neptune Moons.
Intuitively ~ encapsulating his own Time, in looney tunes.
Resonance with energy fields ~ Living Is for the Present.
Intensity > swimming in Warhol's factory, jet Jacuzzi.
No Precedents ~ at the Wonderwall.
*Fame was the Magic * Super Glue*
Loving the absurd
No Denial
No Denial
& No Denial

<u>Oops! Painted Signs</u>
The Familiar * Soup can.
What is it?
Then doing the comics and shoes.
Silk screen Printing as Fine Art decided by whom?
Smiling Marilyn, Jacqui O, Mao and Einstein's show.
Metaphorical, Vernacular of 'Modern' New Culture.
"Controlling the Mind ~ You Control the Person"
And Intention? (licking Tiffany's plate). Be Free
*

<u>Accessible > Call it Experimental Art < if you want!</u>
Operating Against All the Conventions
32 Campbell Soup Cans on Your wall,
depicting the most Common Product ~
And changing the labels; 'Your own Meanings'.
Gov. Experiments in sub-conscious manipulation.
Beginning the Brainwashing on a Mass scale.
Everything has a price, is up for Sale…
In the **Minds** *of the Global Consumer!*
'New Influences' - Branded, Condensed.
Came up with a Great Idea ~ I can See.
Icons of Elvis, Brando, so easy and fun.
Big John Wayne with his faithful Gun!
*

<u>True to U</u>
Unusual * Passion.
William Burroughs' ~ 'Recipe book of Jokes'
A Government 'Think Tank' setting the Values.
Our Values; And You think you can Choose!
Man's Glass Ego ~ spelling, full Contradiction.
"Addicted to Life, fearful of death, of losing, loss"
Contacts, Programs, Associations, Conditionings.
"Born to Live" * "Born to Die"
Make the most of it

Inevitability ~ Recurring Empire?
Conscious of What? Daffodils?
'Make the most of it' > Slogans
Why make others suffer?
Why make others suffer?
Your Mum is slowly
deteriorating next to you
while birds sing
In the early morning…
Connections each moment
A Lifetime of memories
Being happy and sad
Inspiring (conspiring) expiring
Nature's gift ~ to you.
A Fresh Ocean ~
A Fresh Dawn
A Spring Lamb
In fields of bluebells.
Any natural experience
Real not artificial ~
*Reality * beingness*
Intrinsic ~ Trance and dance.
A Universe in a newborn baby
Nature is being nature
to the human eye ~
Capable of building, dazzling illusions
Ignorant Towers reaching to the Heavens ~
Melting Polar Ice caps and burning the rain forest, Planet.
What is a Profitable development for a Global Corporation?
Exploitive Motivation; extinct local, tribal, disappeared human.
Neo-cons and a Military Industrial Complex with Supra-insane
Nationalist tendencies, destruction of all it sees, lost the trees!
No awareness of multi*dimensionalities, holistic eco*bio systems.
We're all in it, synergy together ~ Cosmically, breathing Life

At the Ecstasy Bar with Capt. Alzheimer
Everything is generated by the eternal ~
It's not putting anything into practice
Simply, being, immediately, right now.
"No need to connect ~ we never disconnect"
*"CO2's not driving Earth's heat * Obsession.*
Temperature is always changing phenomena ~
Pointing to the impermanent ~ Oceanic in You.
Not just the wave ~ lost the Yangtze Dolphin today!
Experience being, you are here right now ~ Free, Alive.
Everyone is free but y/our Ego believes it's an Individual,
It, 'I' Is Absolutely Separate > You & Me < Unholistic-ally.
Break out of this shell of dualistic Mind, Transcend it ~
Realise you're not only possessed by Mind ~ Concept.
When we think ~ we become what we are not.
You are no one, but All One ~ that is freedom.
Nothing can effect beyond You.
Your body is a helping friend.
You are what is Intrinsic ~
"Actually you never die"
Takes effort to be bound.
Going into your Mind-Matrix-Program.
The idea that you are definitely an entity.
>> Body-Thinking-Mind is Restricted <<
Your world of experience defines a LIMITED-set
Yet You have no Limit ~ Really there is no You.
"Detachment is not that you should own nothing
but that nothing should own you." All ibn Abi Talib.
You cannot put yourself in only one space in time.
You are total freedom ~ INFINITELY One Space.
You aren't only the person You Think you are.
'Individuality is a Prison' ~ You are immortal.
Unlimited by thought, You are that Freedom.
"Welcome" to everything, It cannot touch you,

No stress, no pain ~ your thoughts, your efforts.
None of this is me, it's all appearance, Mental-Form;
Concepts, Words, Illusions; I haven't done anything.
Allowing it to just be ~ As it is Consciously

*

Mind Projection Is Ultimately a Stream of Consciousness
All limitation is within you ~ Your mental-thought patterns.
All Illusions from a finite Mind-set, reaping what you sow…
Attempts to keep Knowing it are what bind you.
"You Know It by Not Knowing It"
Effortlessly be ~ true reflections.
'Beingness will never die' in reality.
It can't be burnt, that's a great freedom.
The feeling that you are missing out ~ somehow,
is a mind-delusion, that you're always incomplete.
There is a way to freedom, realising this suffering.
That it's all a creation of your Mind ~ Be here now

*

Amidst the Chaos start seeing
the Stars of Truth, a new dawn ~
realizing detachment to the Personal, Me.
In truth nothing happens ~ it's all becoming.
*Eternal existence * You are Inner Beingness.*
"These feelings and thoughts are not eternal"
Everything changes ~ you are as Limitless, no ID.
You, hasn't changed ~ try and get out of Yourself.
Awareness of the changing ~ rainbows within you.
Unknown, No Location

*

Spending your life chasing your thoughts.
Don't believe anything that says,
"You are not complete Freedom"
Can you not be? Yourself ~

Being your experience won't last but Your spirit does ~
"You're always here, haven't been somewhere else"
Your heart Opens ~ the loving feelings flow.
Starting to realise that which will not die ~
Having stress shows, Reality is happening.
'Your Mind is a gust within You'
Your thoughts are a guest too, within You.
It's happening within the infinite changeless ~
Be Conscious, empathetic; how Is Your Beingness?
Krishna told Arjuna, Bhagavad Gita. Chapter, 2.11.
*While speaking learned words you are mourning
for what is not worthy of grief. Those who are
wise lament neither for the living nor the dead*
That's a hard lesson, trying to let go of the Ego.
"You just realised there is no Ego, surreally"
Just an Assumption, look beyond; I Am.
My own experience ~ in this beingness.
Always has been, always will be ~
Observing Objectively, let go of fear.
Intuitive nature * being your true self.
Who's wanting to Control, define Ourselves?
Idea of Association, Relationship, Me, I Am.
There is no one there who needs someone.
You are Free to be ~ Yourself, As One Is.
*

"How can anything be worth this?"
Monkey swinging in a tree, just wanted to live like us.
Ordered not to shoot it. Let them know we understand.
Tapped and chopped all the trees, don't cry Captain!
Looking for Prince Arjuna in the piles of dead bodies.
Reliving another Massacre, what can you do, Ashoka?
"I never understood why Americans came to Viet Nam".
Perfect Fire, brought their inhuman Napalm. "This is wrong!"

Heart Surrendered Beauty
'What is crazy is that people believe what they think is Real'
'Evil ego takes on the Innocent' * Light up this darkness!
Not participating in any artificial Intel/environment.
Paradise is in the eyes of the beholder.
"It's all going on within you"
Loving what is FREE of this ~
Awful, unlawful, Mind-stuff!
"You gotta get out of this place
if it's the last thing you ever do!"
Can't be Unconscious, Consciously….
Can't do Unconscious acts, why would you?
Acceptable, families living on the street in winter?
"You reap what you sow" ~ 'No Self, No Problem'.
Socially Conducive to looking after people; humanity.
What you think is in your head alone not anothers.
All that inhuman profiteering.
Ask any fuckin' Capitali$ta!
*

What is a Master?
'Is this the right time and place for my death?'
Memories are the past, imagination is the future.
Just someone being Alive Now ~
P R E S E N T
Not making it into anything else.
Why are people, desperately homeless?
Distracting from the experience of Life ~
It's not what it used to be, it's what it is now…
Everything is changing throughout the Cosmos
whether we like it or not ~ just our Mind-settings.
Keeping it Omnisciently Real

Chai, Chillum, Chapati
Heard some musical instruments ~ gongs.
Shadow's premonitions, "I think you're gonna die!"
Another kind of line, dividing species on the island ~
All the birds on Bali chasing a charismatic Crown Cockatoo.
Meteor lodestones flying in Magenta, magnetic fields of you.
Parachuted into the Middle of the barren desert.
Alignments of nutmeg more valuable than Gold.
Getting high frequency, bringing back the Spice!

*

Spice Island Songbirds
"I'm gonna buy a ticket."
On top of a Pyramid for the 2012 Solar Eclipse.
Need to laugh ~ Mystical frequencies
Sounds you can touch, you can feel.
My heart fell to my feet, I didn't want to hear it.
Carried an Artificial brain from Outer Mongolia.
A Computer Is * Smart Alien Intelligence.
And a heart is full in Love.
Opening of a vital Chakra
wants to smile ~ beautiful

*

It'll pull you In
She came crashing into my Universo Parallelo.
Created by Nature ~ bouncing on Steroids.
You gotta practice what you pump!
"She'll fuck you for a bag of chips".
Soap Bar, Council house smoke!
War, Ignorance, Loss and Pain evolving to the next step!
H A P P Y * D A Y S * Psy*channeling * Liquid Visions ~
Defining of the Devabara Yuga. "If you want to run this
by an Oligarchy then you got a fight on your hands bud."
Your biological system is being ~ Bombarded!!!

Energy * A Golden Quantum Opportunity

Misused, accused, abused, unable to get a job. A traveller
on the outside looking in, no stable employment references.
Using your 'Id' to drop out of the Mind, took a long holiday!
"Good You had a different Program" being downloaded as...
Who makes these definitions based on what assumptions?
Most of us go Unidentified, Misdiagnosed, Unrecognised,
except for paying taxes. Controlling Security threat records.
Foreseeing 50%, 250,000 marriages a year end in divorce?
The other disasters and personal tragedies all went by too.
Your emotional crises, just crazy, you being pissed again!
Let's be detached, reflecting other species in this Universe.
What is the point of being here, anyway? 'To realise the
differences between the Material and Spiritual Realities'
Have to do it by living it ~ not Projecting Mirrored Images!
Within your sub-atomic heart; not focusing all your desires
on Your body, Id-Ego-Mind. Being Sense-Consciousness,
of your disorders, pains, cravings, hates and expectations!
Realise a body will die and your essential energy continue.
How to recognise this phenomena of such a powerful Maya ~
Illusions, given us as the Truth by unnatural, Political/religious
exploiters of Inequality, Violence, Fear, Ignorance, Insecurities.
In Asia there's philosophies, such as the Vedas, Bhagavad Gita,
having an essential Insight of Spiritual not only Materialistic life.
Dhamma is the infinite force within us, for us to be Self-realised,
to be connected to boundless, Universal energy as other lifeforms.
We can witness by insight Meditation such as a Vipassana Bhava.
Bhakti, devotional service to Transcendent Spirit, becoming aware
of our different Consciousness' vibrations. We are not this Mind-set,
this dictating ego's matrix grip of reality, which is Conditioning us to
absorb the Identity of any 'disorders', so you'll stay Attached in this
Relationship and so under the Control of any manipulative Authority.
Thereby providing your shared values instead of Liberating yourself.
*Be the Conscious Observer, that 'I am' * As It Is, feelings flowing free*

Its Realities

Knowledge is Power to plant an organic seed of truth.
Driver of a spaceship which you are, invoking Satguru.
In the world, not of it, breathing on top of a Lotus pod ~
Don't have to be in that World, don't believe in Palaces.
The Heart gets Reprogrammed > Reprogrammed by...
You see with Compassion, day by day, each moment.
They make you turn on yourself until you hate yourself.
Or help you onto their path! Amygdala's deeper fractal.
A Mystical gathering of Minds ~ Inner Space
Humans don't control the World.
We're going into another realm,
humanity's not going to stop us.
Government's successfully muzzled the justice system!
"It was only for the gold but I wasn't ready for it."
She lights up ~ "Listen, about last night..."
She knows a good noodle place and
she can whip a man with her tongue.
Mad dog's sister from Port Said.
A head for our Hippocampus ~
Come out from in front of the Limbic
not from behind, come from the light.
"Eternity is looking me right in the face." Who is in your heart?
Release the bondages, seeing through the Hypothalamus ~
Under Monsoon skies on deserted beaches. A good way to
get out from under this cortex; unmasking demonic elements.
Machiavelli's Psychopathic Prince, flying his own Private Airbus.
It's a legal bribe my Lord! Have to have a Clear Mind, Opening
Connected, she's humming on your wavelengths ~ together.
Soul to Soul Windows ~ Now we're planing above the flesh.
See it for what it is; they're Manipulating the whole Universe
only for their own ends. We got along with the Homeboys.
Never goin' to be in that gang, always an outsider.
Now I am free ~ don't want to put it into words

"Oh it's good to be Alive!"
Why don't You take 'Possession' of those phenomena?
Strobe lighting every bite of colour in dusky, Olive fields.
"You had a Different Program that's why you had to go
travelling through a density of red cubism. Likes & dislikes.
Introspect, Order your disorder. You break it, you bought it.
Trust is hard, very hard to find and get back, ma Cherie ~
Your mood swings and behaviour drove me fuckin' Mad!
Thankfully I've had some Vipassana Insight Meditation.
Plus knew of Krishna, Spirituality in the Bhagavad Gita.
Where did you get your Normal cultural Programming?
Which Government sponsored, educational Establishment?
'Brainwashing' another reason NOT to define oneself as…
by any brand label, put it all in a bigger * Cosmic context.
Don't get caught by any of Your 'neurological disorders'.
Don't get Captivated by any desires ~ there's a Big list!
Connections, Inter*Relations do you feel Undercurrents?
Do you Realise your True Self from genetics in Spirals?
Up into the Spiritual Sky, not a Materialist Universe dear!
Humanity is changing ~ has a dying body & eternal spirit.
You're separated from your godhead by Maya of Illusion.
A covering, a veil, a mirage, your Ego-self is in distress ~
All part of it, consciousness of the Senses giving you pain.
And your attachment, believing it exists in the body & Mind.
Let that delusion go, let your disorders dissolve into infinity.
The Mix
*

Ultimately regardless of the Myths, religions, we are only
specks in the infinite universe * The 'Tao butterfly effect'.
"Wise wo/men lament neither for the living nor the dead."
Don't get caught in the illusion of ADHD; however Real!
How to realise this in your world of suffering & delusion?
Words are easy, this pain is unbearable & the pills help!
Realise the finite Material world & infinite Spiritual world.

<u>Nice is to be nice</u>
don't you reckon, why be Miserable?
That's the dream ~ BE HAPPY
Sometimes ~ you gotta let go.
Soul within Soul, that's why you can't cheat.
Who you gonna lie to? Breath out is death.
Delusional but it helps you get detached ~
Finally You witness the delusions, smoking!
The Divine forgives even the most fucked up ~
Shiva eats them alive, eats gurus, eats galaxies.
The destroyer is Time ~ it's his energy, he is....
the Lord of Time, for the new spirits to come in.
The Godfather, Sadhus, roaming in a black Mercedes.
Meditating in Crematoriums with skulls and marigolds.
Meditation on being 'dead', letting go of the body suit
until next time; "Who I Am " release ~ now what?

*

<u>It's a Corporation with a Parrot</u>
It's just a Mask, "It's just a curtain,
if you don't know it's a curtain ~
You don't want to go through it."
Swami, one who masters the senses.
Even the Government has to Bow to Krishna.
Shiva takes the lot, Indian tunes, he's havin' a laugh,
Sit there and take it, there's no one to help you.
As far as you know ~ buy a tola or enter there.
Karma, fight your own case with God.
"Use and abuse, mate." ~ "I can't accept that!"
Where there's angels there's devils.
Beautiful living in Perfect Goa ~
In a Paradise with you darling.
Full inspiration in your eyes
Full Love in your heart

Psychedelic Playground
"I believe in marijuana to the Max!"
Yoni ~ fucking the divine * mystery.
What you think are your thoughts are only yours,
not what other people will perceive. Amazin brain!
'Make the most of what life puts in front of you'
You are the Invisible man, you don't exist in her affections.
She switched it off, be the silent witness, a new language.
Reaching for the dreads of daddy Shiva and aunty Kali!
Laying at the feet of Krishna, hearing the growling wolf.
"We got five senses and Thinking, isn't one of them!"
My car talks, it says, 'seatbelt' and my body reacts.
'Indulge in cow smuggling and you will be killed'
"We want to search your house for Jews!"
Or they will crucify you!
*

Bio*Orgcosmic
The Reality you bring
with you ~ making Love.
Inter*stella glistening, iridescent Space chariot.
Exploding, Golden Auroras ~ well worth the wait
*

Global Phenomena
But Is it coming from the heart? "It's not for you, it's to give!"
The simple facts, the simple truth, a cure for depression.
I have to fill in the blanks ~ a catalyst for change.
"That's what makes the world go around ~
Being essential change ~ same, same.
Behaviour sane, sane, different, original.
You gotta be careful what you believe in.
Knowing is ~ My Love makes me Happy.
We get away from the World and Create
something beautiful between ourselves

Debt Slaves
Black man sold black wo*man
to Arabs and white slavers.
Political Correctness
Hypocrisy, heresy and bigotry.
Sociopathic man's kleptocrat casino.
"Do you want anyone telling you
what to believe?" "No."
"There you are then!"
All roots lead you to the same place.
They'll all die ~ what's the difference?
Create your own Happy home in the World.
"I don't get a buzz from seeing farmers
breaking their backs all day, do you?"
Learn about You.
He learnt what hurt him and didn't want to hurt them.
What they didn't know will be explained to you ~
Changed their reactions ~ to the rings of Saturn.
*

Terror Bight
Get a job as Jesus.
Holy Fuck!
"I don't believe in Kings…
or Queens or Pentagons.
I believe in Unicorns & dragons
Absolutely
*

Honey Shaman
Yes we all believe in Love but be aware of the Apsara not Dakshini.
Coked up, narcissistic, selfish, egoistic, deceitful, vampire monster!
You can always tell a perfect ballerina.
Can't beat a bit of idol worshipping.
Back in the cage fucker!

Societal Breakdown
Training them in survival skills, to overcome REAL FEAR!
"Having to rely on yourself mate!" (especially for the ladies).
"Someone's gotta take charge!" blah blah blah; enter Parvati.
Disappearing into the woods or hiding in a cellar, flight or fight!
Defending yourselves and other people you love ~ to death.
Who's building luxury Nuclear bunkers under the golf course?
Who's been in preparation for the coming Apocalypse, Now?
Experts at Forecasting the Future direction of their own game.
Had another stash buried in the back garden, hidden from viral Zombies.
Regular life streams living ~ or demons coming with fire, flood and blood?
"In the event of a Global disaster; a water filter, gas mask and a tomahawk!
Willfully misinterpreting TRUTH, paying extra dementia taxes to the Barons.

*

Gallery Lot
'A Stream of Consciousness ~
for $150,000 on Sale at Auction!
"Bought by an anonymous buyer on the phone from..."

*

Cog 366: dire tribal
"She can hang out with me ~
And bring her girlfriend, dude OK!"
Like when you got your face between someone's legs,
You don't have to worry about language!
There's obviously men gassing their inadequate wives.
And setting them on fire, raping underage, virgin brides!
Not lookin' for a girlfriend, why not? Feudalistic bigotry.
A Brazilian woman, pistol and a Bible
strapped to her pussy, an open book!
Ready to be written on ~
She's lookin' for a relationship.
Cruising attitude, remote control

<u>Notice >There is no TV</u>
"Normally center of Home-Life, Programming Patterns.
Coming right to you, directly into Your Living rooms!
You've got no phone, no car, no woman, not painless,
a mess. When I think about my aches then I'm in Pain!
They don't want the Populace turning on to Class ABCs.
We still think everyone knows that shit but no they don't!"
'Perfect Propaganda', making Romantic, mystical poetics.
Apparently the Chinese don't want to be like that either.
Take your pick >'Dynasty' or 'House of Flying Daggers'.
He fell in Love with Zhang Ziyi's facial expressions ~
These myths touch something in the human heart.
Even the billions in China fall at her pure, seductive gaze.
But why do they eat Tiger meat and have slave children?
"It's propaganda for Beijing like any Police State here".
OK a fantastic production, Imagine lesbian porn next!
Where's their 'InOut' franchise & you've hit the Jackpot!
Yeah, not bad for a white girl, from KlukluxKlan Alabam.
Can have such subtle contradictions in this Coliseum!
*
<u>Type Cast</u>.
If Tommy Lee had gone after their man, Osama Bin...
they would have got him after six weeks. What would
a Sultan's son have said then, to wash his hands of their
blood, yet they continue to support these medieval thugs!
What have they done except squander this black gold pot?
Supporting the biggest Reptiles. devouring whole, Planet Earth.
These are the conspirators' hidden hands controlling death, debt,
disease, famines, poverty, Wars; selling their weapons of Mass -
Destruction from their Palaces, Castles and Mansion Houses
to applause, of their Sociopathic, pompous fornicating lackeys,
with greediness for morals and horror in their withered hearts.
They rule us yet the protectors of society squirm in Obeisance.
No Justice, bypassed in the cause of whose National Interest!

Overriding any who object to their flagrant misuse of Power.
He always gets his fugitive, at least in Hollywood but not this
Princeling of Darkness with his kith and kin and other folks!
At this 'Constitutional' Regalia; Mafia Rule the roost and are
above all laws, plundering this Earth and humanity to death!

*

Scorpions in the Rialto, Dead End Scraps.
Conquistadors in luxury, Private Jets with Swiss Bank Accounts
and Super Yachts, with Suites at the Ritz; mad, blazing, Puppet
Presidents to wage War, on whomever they want to obliterate!
Just have to throw them some bone$ for their Fire Arm$,
which brings only terror while they $uck at $atan's nipple!
"Then the Attorneys turn up and the whiskey starts to flow"

*

Lost in my Trip
It's all an Optical Illusion ~
Is that the conclusion, Baba?
"It's more than criminal, it's diabolical!"
You can't locate anything in a lost brain.
Is it mental illness or human behaviour?
*Bring it on ~ we still got **SLAVE** on our backs!*
She became a standup comedienne in Cambridge!
"I'm not swimming across the river for a sheep Baba"
Telling the Truth about her Sociopathic, narcissistic Mother
In Law.

*

A Lost Pop Star ~ It's all happening Inside
"One of the greatest attributes in life is not to give a fuck about you
or what You thought." "It doesn't matter what people think or say
about You" "Have a nice life" that's OK, a friend told me that one.
It's not apathetic, just do your Passion ~ live your life...
If you're not doing that, you're being someone's Martyr.
Do whatever you're doing, don't give a fuck about it bitch!
No apologies, be Conscious ~ closure; have a nice day.

Freedom again

A nice Chinese woman ~ from Mecca Avenue, SE15.
walked around the Kaaba, with her rainbow Parapluie.
"Not to be dictated to by 'non-decadents', as long
as it doesn't violate someone else's free will ~"
"Yeah, he said that on the way from Magic Mountain"
"Do that I will is the whole of the law." Even Sharia?
"As long as your will does not transgress another's"
*

Now ~ it's already happening

"I always said I wouldn't do anything to a woman
my wife wouldn't do." "Night blooming Jasmine,
spray it in her pussy ~ there's God right there!"
'Biological Imperative' - "Instinct Usurps desire"
"Don't need to connect or disconnect with anything"
That's the Big lie. Continue feeling ~ consciously.
"I like being in the Now" ~ that's where eternity is
No karma, no past or future, being in its Present.
Another Man-Made Concept to do what?
Linear time-sets ~ not a Vertical Sun set!
You're in eternity * in the infinite Now ~
When they realise, that Mind is unreal,
they can't be controlled anymore
*

Beyond the Green Zone

Laughing and dancing all the way through Peru.
"I want you to stay but I'm asking you to leave."
Sanctioned another veiled threat to the Lotus heart ~
Fear of letting go, take a walk inside your infinite Space.
Orbiting the 3rd dimensional galaxy

Chain Reaction Plug-ins!
The many Influences of a Brain Washing.
Diamonds are not a girl's best friend, but
Hitachi's Magic Wand or Jessica's rabbit.
That's the story of my life ~

*

"It's not for you, it's for you to give again!"
"If you want to understand someone's mind listen to their words, if you want to
know their heart watch their actions" No person's actions can ever be predicted
or be blamed. I don't know if you can know someone's mind ~ do I even know
what mine is capable of? I guess after so many years I have an Idea of what is
right or wrong in my holistic world. Do I know how other people arrive at that
point; so many of us are good at role playing and who am I to judge what
another human has experienced, denying any compassion? Maybe if I watch
my mind and my heart then at least I will be true to my*self and other's
seeming mad, ignorance won't be so devastating. 'Innocence is bliss ~
Or as Sadhguru says, "Life becomes beautiful when you are willing
to give it all and you don't care what you get." Om Shanti Shanti.

*

Implanting Dennis' Hopper Pill
You design golf courses, I design notebooks for expensive hotels.
Total Recall, Blade Runner; why take time off work, a vacation
when we can give you virtually the exact same experience?
It's just like you did it yourself, "I'm your man." Hip noetic ~
A third wave passed, he made Jimi Hendrix Martini Cocktails.
Marilyn Monroe Quaaludes, Blue Pill, Diazepam, Tamazepam.
"The memory's there but I can't remember it." "Just Accept It."
Venus' Secret, "It's the Universe" for my Agent Provocateur.
"I don't think any two Individuals can share ~
the same visions otherwise we'd all be one chakra"
'All things change and we change with them'
Light * no light * Star bright

*Hrsikesa * Master of the Senses*
New Phoenix rising in your wing mirror Image.
Deconstruction ~ disconnection, deconditioning.
To Transcend its Thinking-Mind, try Insight Meditation.
We all have to die of something, somewhere at some time;
being the identification of your cravings, desires and disorders.
Ideas of Mind, My Mind, Your Mind, illusion, delusion, are Thoughts.
Complete 'Self' confusion only exists to be Transcended in the east.
But in Western culture, Mind is the raison d'etre, the pinnacle of all!
To be a Materialist, Egoist not Spiritualist, metaphysicist, naturalist.
There is Theocratic Religion with a history of Inquisition; Si, Galileo?
Not rising above the predatory Mind, for the killers of the Cathars!
Their Heaven on Earth is to own Empires; 'In God we Trust'; what?
A boundless Space beyond Mind per se for them is Inconceivable.
An ability to be Self-Realised, Self-Recognised, is heresy, anarchy.
In Ancient lands this Spirit quest is what makes us Unique in Nature.
As humans not animals, Angels or other frequencies of density ~
Being Self-conscious of our Opened Mind is our human destiny.
Transcendence into Cosmic realms, Space ~ here and now.
As described by Krishna to Arjuna in the Bhagavad Gita.
Western powers want us reeling, whirling, separated,
'disordered' in our own Mind, to obey their command!
Controlling energy by Insanity, can't Step out of Order, or!
No true sense of Awareness, Meditation, Tao, a holy cow!
No true Psychic, mystic spirit feeling bliss in nothingness.
Doesn't mean we follow white rabbits down fantasy holes
or turn into psychedelic, crystal crocodiles with big smiles.
Or talk to little green trolls living in the lush, fecund Flora.
Or happily whisper to Venus, lovingly inside your heart ~
Don't be fearful, stressed, anxious, worried or depressed.
These disorders exist to go beyond, into self-realised bliss.
From Master Ego's pains, sufferings, Ignorance, tragedies,
we break! Surrender, become humble, let it go, be in tune ~
with Prana, Life force in every leaf ~ under Shiva's moon.

WOWIE

Love energy fields, Consciousness is an amazing high.
"Nothing will really change until we change ourselves ~"
Enemies are in the Mind being fed all the hate experience.
Something to make your ego feel stronger and crazier!
"Hate is too big a burden to carry" ~ It's all here now.
"The Queen is still making people into knights!"
It's Not what you do but how you do it...
On an empty tropical beach, inside your heart.
Part of conditioning, 'Longing to reign over us'
A wild animal doesn't want to do tricks ~
Reward and Punishment, making it a slave!
Getting Materialist, the Mind is Self-seeking.
It doesn't see beyond things ~ wants more
things in order to be satisfied but never will!

*

"What will be waiting for us when things go BA BA* B O O M?"
Going above the ground, all suited up,' what will you happen to see?
"You certainly need a toilet when the Bombs start flyin...."
Wolves, sheep and sheep dogs, survival of the fittest on Survival Planet.
Who said that and is it true? Ask Mr. Orwell or Sadhguru of its veracity.
I'd rather stay with my family to the end, being in the spirit of all living things.
Mad Max with good, bad and extremely ugly Sheriffs, for urban survivalists!
'Nuclear war is a possibility that most people prefer not to contemplate'.
See it in the right light * Magical reflection, seeing other dimensions,
the eternal flame ~ through Your Mind's eye * dissolving with Love.
Entering exploding mushrooms in a higher state of Consciousness!
Bringing Prana Life Force down into the Core, spinning your Vortex!
On the plateau of Progression, it does have some true meaning ~
Philosophy of Life, wiping out Karmic debts, a victim's mind-games!
Hell on Earth * Heaven on Earth, we're just a light body ~ channel.
Changing our DNA; spirals of light ~ reflections from Inside Out.

They're Killers - My Peasant Slave Dogs!

Living is a Form of Art ~ Fight for freedom, sunny warrior.
You are/I am inside the pyramids. No regrets! WHY would you allow that, such
servitude, taken absolute power over your life? "We had no choice"; obviously!
'Ius primus noctis', Le droit de Seigneur accepted as real. On Your honeymoon;
first he took your innocent, newly married lover, your wife and fuckin raped her!
"The Nazis won the War and the Germans lost it!"
Enslaving Humankind through money and debt.
The dark forces cannot exist in Consciousness ~
Who is ruling this Planet by Fear and thuggery?
The Devil has Acct # BIS. Palace, das Oberland.
Pharaonic aristocrats with castles up in the Alps.
Worshipping the Sun God ~ Ra over Lake Como.
Knock, knock, who's there creating all these wars?
Lune de Miel, licking DNA. off your virgin bride's clit.
Who are these Templars sitting atop of the Pyramid?
Breaking the Octogon codes of the widow Isis' sisters.
Going on a global looting spree with the Swiss Fascists.
A genocide of 50 million people with their Skullduggery!
Ask yourself who is financing Islam-fascism today?

*

CULLING * CLAIR * VOYANCE

*Whose up for a bit of science fiction*Nasha!
Masked Pharaohs still in control of their slaves!
When you look at the state of the World today - conspiracy.
The Planet is bountiful, wonderful, beautiful, ALIVE for all of us.
We have six people with the wealth of half the total planet's population.
Thirteen oligarchic families completely ruling the Earth for themselves!
There are indescribable inhuman, unnatural disasters and devastation.
Coked, Sociopaths with Power are making the wrong decisions; obviously!
Do they have another Agenda 21 to continue starving, killing, flaying us all?
Cruelty; where is Consciousness ~ empathy, humanity not enslavement?

*cling cling * ching ching*
Channeling Magic Horus ~
Taking all the Servants with you.
It's gone a bit too far, too Materialist; what a Megalomaniac!
A Happy 'Divine' Emperor who conquered himself. "At least
Robin Hood wore a mask!" Struggling against the odds-Death.
You just meet it, then what do you do? Returning to our source.
Thrown out of jail, embrace the light ~ Everlasting Life.
Proper Prana Training, he's been flying off.
He's got the point, opening the Pineal gland.
*~ **Spiritual beings in a physical world** ~*
All part of the Oneness, balances the Mind.
Pulsating Crystals, I saw your heart glowing.
Psychic portrait, about Variations, Vibrations.
*
They go together ~ Complimentary
"The eagle has landed" ~ into Om, elemental ether.
Keeping us tuned into Electric-Kool Aid Acid test!
Smoke, pills, MDMA. whatever it is.
One day Love & trust will walk out.
You're stuck in the head, it's a trip.
Into another dimension, Merkaba ~
Spirals coming from a Heart Chakra.
*Totally Loved * up pussy in ecstasy*
*
just the case
Took me to her version of 'Dolce Vita'.
Into a surreal ~ Infinity swimming pool.
Going to Bamboo forest, Monkey Valley.
Overwhelmed ~ by this beautiful land.
Manifesting and Multiplying, honouring.
All One Mind ~ lines in the blowing sand.
*One * Spirit*

Life is a breeze
Definitely an old soul.
All you can do is pray
that your kids stay safe.
Jupiter is all about expansion
My time to fly ~
Had my Mercury in Sagittarius.
My Venus sits in Scorpio
*Hot as fuck * Planet*
at my birth Scorpio rising.
I'll see you another day
*

Keeping It Real
Very emotional
Very Sentimental
Got a handle on it
Hanging onto the Moon
In the moment
Always hated the walls of a stable.
Tried to put me in a box.
"I'll kick it down!"
I had to dance the energy
*

They'll Stump it up
using their noggin…
I've got them on the 'op
Had me twitchin' ~
"He's a Baba for sure, for sure, for sure"
We want the bollocks in little baby Bill.
'Mr. Delightful'
Do you think they got Cider in Goa
or Skyrocketing Avatars off Xanax?

They love their Candy (Coke)
"Never known such a Twisted Bastard in my Life!
Mad as Fuck but I love 'em; can you explain that?
A Fuckin' handful, as if it's a Crime to a Freeman.
"Don't exaggerate, she hasn't been raped!"
Knocked on the wrong door......
Nightmares you'll take to the grave.
No guilt left, all gone.
All been dissolved
*

Pick from the well of a Funky Diva
"The Universe gives me £200 in my hand
And a job I loved to do ~
Sandblasted the Front door...
Found you in an Elizabethan Manor.
Had a Meltdown, scrubbed up well
And got myself to the big house.
Sitting at the Big Table
Lush to some people ~
Our Universe is Not for Sale"
*

Sumerian Pill Blaster
Civilisation started on rivers ~
"I'd never seen anything like it!"
They worked the river...
"To meet her is to Love her,
just get a Rose crystal, man"
What a Perfect, Precious Gem.
The Pearl is the New Moon
came on the Violet Ray ~
There are the Big Angels
She's Vibrating closer to me.
The light coming back
She's always been a Rocket!

Totally Mother Earth
"It was a very nice home ~
And I also visited other people
with nice houses."
Treating yourself to Goa ~ Really
because every part of you deserves it.
Miss Superstitious
A Witch, this or that or the other.
I'll blind her with my Might
I think you're right.
"I've Power of light, I'll take her down!"
You Fuckin' Tyrant.
"Listen to you ~
*

Leave the Universe with that
Don't get drawn in ~
Clear where she's coming from.
"I can't hack it!"
Have the Mind-set
to leave it alone ~
Let it Work
Yeah come on sister!
Break that Scowl to smithereens.
"And you can fuck off!"
Told me all the things I wanted to hear
And I saw through it.
And I gave up the factory job
"I've got to resign ~
I'm suffering from heartache.
And I've got to go off to Mexico
got to sell my car..."
"Just tell me what you need
doing at the Light Centre"

Playing with Tarot
Ruled by Uranus and Venus
Perfect Revolutionary Sparks
She's golden ringed Saturnalia not saturnine.
A Humanitarian water carrier ~
Floating in the more rumbling Planets
I Know I've been blessed ~
What a total fuckin' headfuck!
If you've things badly aspected.
"Home is where the Heart is"
doesn't mean 4 walls....
30 years to make an orbit
"I feel" * "I feel"
Purely emotional ~
COUNTER * BALANCE
*

It's dying to get itself
Attached, it's got to have it ~
"My experiment with Truth" Is changing
"How do we know ~ going with the flow"
"Under her monster hood, couldn't get over that one
Anyway!"
*

Gopi Govinda
Rock hard fairies ~
(not) Angels with Attitude.
Once you're channeled
You lose a lot ~
Spontaneous self-expression.
Subjective*Objective, the Observer,
to keep that Mind Completely off it.
Don't let it wander or be distracted,
let it reflect its own pool from Inside.

<u>What are we doing on Alta Mountain?</u>
Wow, 'the psychedelic dandy of the Flower Power'
Most people were Out of their Minds
At that Time ~
Perfectly in-Synch Not Psychic imprisonment >
Those Star spangled banners burning in the atmosphere.
Distorted, horrors, good ol' US. was inflicting on Viet Nam!
And Magical metaphors for flexible, Hendrix's guitar riffs ~
completely natural, playing Against extremes of Madness!
The good die too young ~ in Hanoi schools and Haiphong,
And later in a basement of the Samarkand Hotel, Kabul.
"If a voice has character, if you sound like Yourself
And you sound like you mean it ~ its soul resonates!
Not fertilising a Charade of servitude." "Yes Master!"
That Unholiest of Wars, must have cost us a Bomb!
Renunciation ~ fruit shack at a full Power Ashram

*

*<u>Perfume * Signals</u>*
Found her on a psychedelic Rock
growing irresistible little Orchidées ~
carried her away, nature mating in midair.
Female mimicry, sexually deluded another male,
*clinging to another * It's all a Universal miracle.*
High up in the canopy spreading gleams of Life.
Human beams of light ~ nothing more to say…
*Sensing * Sensing*

*

<u>Biggest Crime</u>
Like fuckin' up the Garden of Eden.
Unconsciously, what's your excuse?
Forgiveness ~ they don't have a f…..g clue!
Divine Super-Intelligence is seemingly Alien.
Frequencies speaking through Planet Earth.

Wheat Fields into Styrofoam Cups

We're like mad Bulls with a Red Flag!
Perfume would be wasted on them.
DNA. florets of spectacular nectar…
Night bloom pollinating Venus' Moon.
Being drawn inside her wet labia ~
Ambrosia feeding, longer tongues,
drinking from their deeper nectaries.
Tuning fork, stamen's right vibrations.
Synchronous, Honeysuckle discharge ~
Essentially using humans for its own survival.
Partnering ~ probing with the full length…
Inviting
*

We Share the Same Planet

'Dharavi', Mumbai, the largest slum in Asia! A worry -
WIFI. beams of radiation on electro ~ hyper sensitivity.
Biological effects downloaded on your innocent children.
Government Exposure, making Brain controlled Zombies.
And Corals, 1% of heated Ocean, but 25% of Marine life!
Of course they fought over the remaining, productive soil.
UV. light shines up night insects & black faced marmosets.
Revealing the Scale of our Ignorance - We are disastrous!
Pumping a billion vapour trails, crossing an Unknown line.
Ocean is still a Mystery, depth of 7 miles; And Jet streams?
Along the walls is the evidence ~ recognising the suffering!
90% of cells in the body are bacteria ~ We still have a lot of
resources on the Planet, naturally, to be exploited by humans!
Bye Panda, chelo Tiger, Orangutan, on the road to extinction!
Destroying Bio*diversity ~ sea otters, Pacific krill, sea urchins,
whales, rhinos, bees, giant Kelp forests, equatorial virgin jungles.
Exploding * holistic Species, we're not living in Isolation anymore.
Limits of exposure, Meteor Impact, Interconnection, acceleration!

Alien Venus' Eroticum with an Osiris Crane
Rap, Capitalism, Conspicuous Commercialism, Consumption.
Based on, heavily influenced by industry; Acid rain emissions.
Eco-bio-chemical systems and destination of local driver ants!
The Global damage by humans, ½ million different species dead.
Plastic, Microscopic bacteria swimming inside a Blue Whale ~
50,000 killed each year. The Economic resource of Gorillas?
Rwandan wastelands, needs 8 square miles for spotted owls.
Save the forest, save Animals; who put prices on their heads?
Can't regenerate it at any Time or Control what's destroyed!
Vast over harvesting, butterfly cooperative, $1 per poupea!
20 million Seahorses are killed each year ~ Un$ustainability!
Males & females mating for life, gatherings at night, Living Planet!
Carbon dioxide threat of Pollution, heating the seas, 1-5 degrees.
"Human effect like a modern Meteor collision with the Dinosaurs!"
Or Chinese Medicine's diagnosis of a tearful Tiger! WTF!!!!
*

Well Hallo Dolly and Who the F… is Responsible for this?
*'The Tall Poppy Syndrome' * too clever for their own good!*
Reflection of their distress in a 'Culture of Excellence'.
Joke, 'just don't get sick in August' & No Fault Divorce'
We didn't recognise them as Predators but now we do!
Slaughtering a population of 5000 to 10,000 hedgehogs.
Trees, birds, ten times more destruction of, than creation!
Out of control, ripping off too much ~ to develop what, $?
Finding every last shrimp in the $ea with Hi Tech. Why?
Introducing Killer Snails, exterminating native Hawaiians.
Nature is creating the air, water, our environment for Free.
Do you want to live as a Blade Runner with Android sheep?
Human viruses whenever settling on islands or grasslands.
The destruction of habitats, of $pecies, biological Hotspots.
Massive Agricultural losses, on the Verge of mass Extinction.
Six thousand plants once, nowhere else on Earth, lost Paradise.
The richest variety of Life that our children now will never see ~

Pure Union Unborn (of time)

Delusions, fucked-up, lustre, desire, greed, selfishness,
bullshit, Ignorance, denial, hate, resentment, hypocrisy,
Negativity, jealousy, misunderstanding, suffering, pride,
rejection, loss, disdain, irresponsibility; Pure philosophy.
'Shrutti or Smrtti' coming to me from heaven in dreams.
Amazing, complete Identification with a given technique.
A set of Rules, path, list, a One and only meaning to Life.
"To be or not to be?" Which says be now ~ celebratory free.
Don't be attached yet fully in contact to Cosmic Conscious.
A Paradox ~ letting it go to nowhere. A nervous breakdown
in rain clouds over the Highlands of some inner Awareness.
An emotional breakdown in a brain full of pained Poisonings.
Feeding it ~ Illusions of air, bread, water, body, a sunrise,
a sunset, day, night, whole stories of being; drop the lot!
Identification is everything, all the time of your existence.
Reflecting through your Mind's thoughts ~ Oceanic waves.
Is there something Real in an illusion > of this experience?
Ultimately there is no illusion, it is all the boundlessness ~
Passing through all the gates, inside*outside of salvations.
Yins Yanging, Nirvana I Chinging on a Pathless path ~

*

Mutants visiting the Mall, No Hope Square, Universal ~
St. Station; Temptation in Eden, Cranach's Adam & Eve.
The Power of Suggestion gone with Reverse Psychology.
Enjoying the friendly fire, from your Commanding officer!
"Rejected the horizontal Perspective, point of ref. in Time,
for a fluid, singular surface, modulated by colour, texture.
Free, being here now, abstract art wave of Free Association.
From Inside going through the 3D bark, depth of synchronicity.
Following his downfall, the Palace became unrelated, unable
to face itself, hedonist, lavish entertainments, neurotic central.
"How can I Trust you again?" You never want to lose that darling!
It doesn't come back ~ nerves in the energy centre of your heart.

Phoenix Spirit of Creative Freedom
"Suggesting a loss of fixed Identity....
eruptions from within the Individual of ~
suppressed anxieties & Liberating Powers!"
Meaning the No Meaning of 'Anarchy'
Unfreeze children in an Unfree society.
Took some Inspiration from believing ~
"The child in Man is all that's strongest,
most receptive, most open and Unpredictable."
Inspirational Shiva Moon and Miro's Peinture-poeme.
'Un étoile caresse la sérénité d'une negresse'. C'est vrai?
'Surreal, disconcerted Mind, dysfunctional logistics'
Instincts ~ appearing on a gibberish sunbeam
*

Elemental Relationship
Full Anarchy in Art, no Rules, Regulations, in the moment!
She subverts established Temporal logic through Slits
of Poetry, dream, Imagery; 'Freeing up the Mind-sets'
'Associations <:> of highly personal, visual language!'
"Just be beingness" beyond, surrealism or anything else.
Let it all go, dissolving Ego realms of projected Karma.
New Insights ~ into human propensity, density, gravity.
Crucifiction etc. defined by 'Psychology', it's All O.K. then!
Dehumanizing conflicts by desensitizing ~Tuning thoughts
into action; 'Archetypes' of Insanity living in tubes of Testes.
TV. brains invented by Freudians! Powers of the Irrational,
*not needing to think or analyse * Realise your whole being,*
letting the Unconscious < No Mind > fly free ` Surprisingly.
Hidden desires 'Obsessional-Possessional' Madness, fell
to Celebrate Total Revolution of Love
*

Uncensored
Creature's Impulses
of the Unconscious

NATURAL PSYCHEDELIC
There's no face to Buddha's vibe.
Telling it Not as the Ego-Me-Mine ~
Just telling it, asking an Innocent heart.
Identity embedded from eating an apple,
then ashamed they had to wear clothes of knowledge!
It starts to feel, Kissing her breasts, writing Love songs.
'This mission is too important to undermine ~
It's becoming more important than Life itself!'
*

Intuitional Archetypes of the Collective Unconscious
"Could someone you know be thinking of ending it all?"
Clear & Conscious, Unconditioned, Loving, Opened Mind.
It's Non-Attachment ~ to the 10,000 petaled Lotus galaxy.
Kahunas Caressing Spiritual Wahinis in perfect delirium.
"Shut up the talkin' Mind; she ran off with a fisherman."
'I think therefore I am, I am therefore I think, deep inside'
'The art of knowing is knowing what to ignore' ~ Rumi.
Horseshit with the Image, go into total Acceptance
*

River with the Colorado Corazon of Sur*reality
Love show, live show off the hook, sorry I drifted off ~
Full of hot desires, full power * blackest nights sparkling
in emerald, crusted eyes she flies without disillusionment.
Timeless multi-dimensionality on an Amazonian dusty road.
Finding natural peoples, finding natural harmony ~ sailing
a boat up Rio Branco, searching for female diamond shoots.
Opening up her petals like a bee * impregnating orchidées ~
Gently going inside with full Shaman inspiration, to the roots.
Feeling divinely to discover sublimely, her raptures in mine!
It's bright at the beach of Supra*Orgasmic Consciousness

Illegal Paranoias ~ swimming into buried treasures
The interiors; acceptance of the intentions; Ok…
I tuned into your glowing show of vibrating vibrancy ~
Attracting me into your vagina * freeing my Obsessions
from consequences of sperm, in a prehistoric life's germ.
Used it for my ecstasy, used me for your sacred pleasure.
Don't worry about what you got, I asked Shiva all about it.
University of Life's Love in Real, Chemical-Eco-Bio Worlds.
Satan made the theatre, so staying hard with snorting Bulls!
Rocket in your pocket, let the butterflies have their Spaces ~
Freedom of Uniqueness ~ changing the things I need to do.
I don't dig holes in the earth anymore; I climb trees, feeling free
no comparisons, symbiosis, use it for y/our benefit ~ Be Wise
*
*

White Lines

You call Right Wrong and Wrong Right, go beyond definitions.
Total Perversion ~ a lie is a lie is a lie, is still keeping on lying.
OCD. "Consumed by Obsession; greed not freed to handle it"
The Plant is telling you, the Planet is begging you, to wake up!
Not consumed by Addiction; it can handle it, can you?
She has the Brain of Brains, Spiritual, sexuality, ecstasy.
Flowing energy ever going higher, up the psychic wire.
Heaven is the Ultimate, that's where children are free ~
*
*

Paradox, concept of Perfection; It's Perfect, no Stress.
"Re-Scramble the Mind, don't use Programming words"
"I have Peace Man, I can't describe it, I am Content."
I'm growing, plants getting the light; no day or night.
Disciplined ~ Surrendering to the Freedom Channels.
Clear Crystal fractals giving holographic sight ~ Vibrating.
"How can I give you more when your cup is already full?"
Constant flowing Cosmic energy * fulfilling Oceans' infinity

*Observation of Conditionality * Dreams of Signorelli*
"Forgotten memories of terror and orgies of Suffering"
Predator, Matrix-thought devoured her soft Pink Shell.
Believe or not believe in infinite Space ~ Mind is Limited; or
Consciousness Expansion and Why? One's own self-analysis.
Attached to the poles ~ liberation is from inside, Your own Mind,
through your own Mind, released from delusions of anyone else.
*

Nailed It!
'As they're putting their cross in that box!'
Let's have a massive human resurerection!
Vote for Peace and Love and Rock and Roll ~
"I'm Sorry!" "What the fuck does that mean mate?"
I Love this guy; "Show no fear in front of the Devil."
Gods, Kings, Moses, Prophets, Inquisitions, Popes, Saudis,
the Oligarchies, Queens, Establishments, Dark Government.
Krishna, Shiva, Kali, NWO. Bilderburgers, Illuminati, Military?
Natureally ~ who's allowing the Free Parties not Enslavement?
Adam and Eve becoming Conscious of their human innocence
*

*PSYCHO * PATHS*
Dark tentacles as seen by non-interventionists; what the fuck is that?
Does anyone pay attention to any of this bullshit? That's created…
It would be ironic if it wasn't so Sociopathy-logical, anthropological!
Where are the Protectors of the natural laws of our Planet Earth?
Who is empowered to condemn these Crimes Against All of Us?
Who are just and courageous to enforce humanity's living truth?
*

Plugged Into her Rocket Socket
'She'll come out dancing for you ~ like the stars at night'
Now everything is new under this spectacular Sunrise!
'Your kisses broke me Free!'
Heart's radiant delight

Mercilessly Cruel Tyrant
No honour, no respect, no merit, graceless Shogun.
Switch off the Thinking; what does it mean?
How much for your body?
How much for your mind?
How much for your heart?
How much for your feelings?
How much for your Spirit?
*Love * Life at all cost!*

*

'Tune in, turn on, drop out'
A mission to defeat the enemy in a Zen garden.
"The time has come to lay down your life ~
for the greater good." "Are you ready to die ninja?"
Kill them all, another diabolical, pure evil massacre!
A leader with sociopathic, schizophrenic tendencies.
To die for your Lord! "Isn't he another Robber Baron?"
It just happens, not really knowing how any of it works.
It comes like that, tuned into those dark frequency ranges.
Protecting Innocence, see the children and their parents!

*

Narcissus' Reflection ~ All Twinkled Up
Without any regret or guilt, self-perception ~
'The most ego pollution not the best solution!'
No feelings of empathy, what a poor person.
It's a good thing to be painless, hard inside?
Another skull tied on for Mother Kali!
Doesn't really care if you lived or died ~
Thrown over a cliff into the crashing sea!
Bottom line not to be pissed off ~
Bottom line to have a clear, open Mind.
Let your will surrender darling.

Qualities of a Sociopath

'Someone who is described as a sociopath will have several traits that set them apart from those with no personality disorders. These traits include: * Lack of empathy - Inability to feel sympathy for others or to understand the emotional consequences of their actions. * Cold, calculating nature - The ability and willingness to use others around them for personal gain. * Shallow emotions - Lack of real emotion in response to events, limited capacity to feel love. * Narcissism - A personality disorder in itself, in which the individual feels strong love and admiration toward themselves (often a defense mechanism against deep seated low esteem). * Grandiose self-image -They might see themselves as someone who is superior to others and sometimes even experiences delusions. A sociopath might see themselves as a fitting ruler of a country or even the world, but might also have delusional beliefs such as seeing themselves as a God or having super powers. * Charming - While the sociopath is unable to fully understand the emotions of others, they are capable and rather highly adept at mimicking them and might appear to be charming and normal at first. * High IQ - Often sociopaths will exhibit a high IQ which they can use to manipulate and plan. * Manipulative - Sociopaths use their superficial charm and high IQ to manipulate others to get their ends, and their lack of empathy allows them to do this with no sense of guilt or remorse. * Secretive - Has little need for others and is highly secretive in their actions. * Sexually deviant -The lack of remorse, guilt or emotional attachments means that the sociopath is happy to have affairs and to engage in questionable sexual activity without questioning their desires. * Sensitive to criticism -That said, like all narcissists, the sociopath will desire the approval of others, will be highly sensitive to criticisms. They often feel they deserve adulation and admiration of the world and might feel victimized. * Paranoid - Often their lack of understanding of emotion along with their incongruous self-view means that they feel a lack of trust and paranoia. * Despotic/Authoritarian - Often the sociopath will see themselves as a necessary authority and will be in favor of totalitarian rule. * Lawfulness - Despite popular belief, a sociopath is not likely to be a problem to the law in later life, but rather will seek to find loopholes, to rise to a position of power, or to move to another area so that their behavior is tolerated * Low tolerance for boredom - Sociopaths require constant stimulation and get quickly bored. * Impulsive behavior - A lack of regret and empathy makes sociopaths more likely to make sudden rash decisions based on the current facts. * Compulsive lying - As part of their façade and as a means to an end, sociopaths are compulsive liars and will rarely speak truthfully, making them hard to pin down.

Sociopaths of course vary in their symptoms and might act differently in different cases. However, their main trait is presenting themselves as having the same empathy, feelings and emotions as others when in fact they lack this emotional capacity. They are thus cold and manipulative and rarely see any problem with their actions. (see egosyntonic)

*

Profile of a Sociopath

A sociopath is likely to have been a 'problem child' and exhibited difficult behaviour when younger. As they grow older they are likely to be highly successful which is a result of their willingness to get one over on their competition and colleagues, a desire and belief in success, and lack of risk aversion. Alternatively, a sociopath might be likely to live on the fringes of society having little interest in people. They could be eccentric and will most likely be independently wealthy. In other words, they will either conquer the system or avoid it entirely. They will of course have few close friends and are more likely to make contacts with those they can use, or those they see as equals and that they can admire. They will tend to be cold and manipulative in

relationships and potentially emotionally abusive, though this might
not necessarily be purposefully vindictive. In all cases though
the psychopath will appear highly intelligent, charming and
charismatic to talk to and it is only careful guardedness
that can uncover their true motivations.

Arranged from: Characteristics of a Sociopath
by Stanley C. Loewen
*

Unconditional Love
Life within a tranquil, Zen garden full of pink cherry, blossom trees.
Makes you realise your own mortality, empathy, telepathy, destiny.
Heart's going deeper in Love with a sociopathic, narcissistic lover.
I should have listened to my dying mother!
Infatuated, sexuality filled with desire,
need, inside a burning, orgasmic fire ~
Lying in her arms feeling happy dreams.
Seduction and tender intimacies, trusting.
Coquettish smiles say, she loves to fuck you!
*

Humanity Is Empathy
Your lack of courage; giving up, insecure, selfish ego,
deceit, resentment, anger, narcissism, fear, greed!
'You can't deny Love, how could You?'
Exactly, that's a very good question…
"Give her what she fuckin' wants!"
*

Money talks (bullshit walks)
'No matter how educated, talented, rich or cool you believe you are.
How you treat people ultimately tells all.' Who are you el Diablo?
How well we treat ourselves, how well we treat all natural Life ~
Love says, "I am everything" ~ Wisdom says, "I am nothing"
Nisargadatta * Consciously :)

Sniffing, Cumming to get you
"I used to know her lovely name,
now I curse her every fuckin' day!"
She's a Luciferian, Starlit black hole ~
A sociopath out cruising after midnight!
A flip-out with a special flirting smile.
Come and get me witch!
*

Primavera mollusk
Tripping down a country lane ~
Arriving in time for Aphrodite's birth.
Coming out of her Cowrie, sea conch.
Going in different directions…
Living in one's own Spiral shell.
"I broke her heart!"
*

Anti-Church's Confessional Censorship, Cherie
"I had to think about the body in order to control it"
Engraved erotic images, texts from Mantuan Palace walls,
with frescoes of sinners stripped of all their original context.
Seduced by her throbbing clitoris inside the Procope café.
And invitations to Philosophers from l'Academie des Filles.
Disgorging Revolutionary pamphlets, filling hot vacuums,
stilling sex ~Totemic forces, through Political Pornography.
'Without remorse we are completely alone', from de Sade's,
Dominance. Found 'La victime' for ridiculing Misogynists and
the preparation of a mob, for the execution of a despotic pair!
Poetical Not Political, does it make sense; why and why not?
Alive is a Spirit World of Tao ~ pure, simple, in essence, now.
Come down to go up, through the fire, to purge wo*man's ego.
Not cosmetically ~ Symbiosis, Synchronically, Cosmically

Democracy Now
Government Plan to Control - the Political Mind! Why bother?
Go surfing, clicking Social media ~ different angles, viewing.
Being intimidated or did you find the guerrilla network news,
not those Medusas? Selling the Wars with General Electric,
NBC.CBS. CNN. Viacom, Foxes embedded in a Pentagon!
"Be not a News Consumer but a Critical Thinker and More"
*

*Kama * DNA * Deva*
Ah, Venus, what of dark, fiery, warring, burning, hot Mars?
Brahma, Shiva, Vishnu, Krishna, Ganesha, Lakshmi, Kali.
"Do You Trust Me?"
"Trust you to do what?"
At the bottom of the garden are her beautiful offerings ~
Red hibiscus ~ the Goddess and flower merging in form.
*

Anonymous
"You can shed tears that she is gone
or you can smile because she has lived.
You can close your eyes and pray that she'll come back
or you can open your eyes and see all she's left.
Your heart can be empty because you can't see her
or you can be full of the love you shared.
You can turn your back on tomorrow and live yesterday
or you can be happy for tomorrow because of yesterday.
You can remember her and only that she's gone
or you can cherish her memory and let it live on.
You can cry, close your mind, be empty and turn your back
or you can do what she'd want. Smile, open your eyes ~
Love and go on."

ABOUT SUNNY JETSUN

Inspired by the sixties, Sunny started traveling the world in 1970.
His spiritual journey on the hippie trail to India took him through ~
San Francisco, Los Angeles, London, Amsterdam, Paris, Vancouver,
Sidney and Kathmandu to Varanasi. His arrival on the sub-continent ~
was the beginning of writing autobiographical verses capturing his travel
experiences, encounters with remarkable people and his quest for self-
realization. Combining experimentation with drugs, sex, rock & roll, art,
meditation, Love and life in general. Sunny started to open up to a multi-
dimensional Universe. He lived the mantra, "Turn on, tune in, drop out"
realising Mind's-illusions, inspired by deeper feelings of holistic nature,
empathy*energy & Space.

Over four decades Sunny has written and published 30 books of poetry,
created over one hundred paintings, traveled the World and considers
his masterpiece to be his daughter. He has spent the past fifteen years
in Goa, India inspired by the freedom to experience and idealism
of human consciousness.

Sunny Jetsun books and art are available on the web at:
Website: www.sunnyjetsun.com
Facebook: www.facebook.com/sunnyjetsun
Amazon: www.amazon.com/author/sunnyjetsun
Smashwords: www.smashwords.com/profile/view/sunnyjetsun

www.ingramcontent.com/pod-product-compliance
Lightning Source LLC
Chambersburg PA
CBHW020507030426
42337CB00011B/275